MW01531750

Our Chown Odyssey

VOLUME I

From Vikings to Venetians

by

Thomas A. Chown II

Donated to Fort Scott
Geneology Society
by Thomas A. Chown
A personally autographed
copy of his family's
progression from England
to Fort Scott to Colorado
and on to Illinois. He was
the great grandson of
William & Mary Chown who
lived in Fort Scott during
the Civil War.   H.P.A.

RitAmelia PRESS

Our Chown Odyssey: Vol. I. From Vikings to Venetians, by Thomas A. Chown II
© 2004 by Thomas A. Chown II

Published by RitAmelia Press
Morriston, Florida

Distributed by Thomas A. Chown
19200 SW 90th Lane Road
Dunnellon, Florida 34432

Edited by Drollene P. Brown
Page design by Shauna H. Graham

Printed by a division of Keithco, Inc.
Ocala, Florida

Printed in the United States of America

All rights reserved. No part of this book may be reproduced, stored in a retrieval system, or transmitted in any form or by any means electronic, mechanical photocopying, recording or otherwise, without the prior written permission of the publisher.

ISBN: 0-9641216-8-9
Price: $20.00

Cataloging-in-Publication Data

Chown, Thomas A., 1943-
Our Chown Odyssey: Vol. I. From Vikings to Venetians/by Thomas A. Chown II
        p.cm
ISBN: 0-9641216-8-9
1. Thomas A. Chown, 1943. 2 Chown, Walter C., 1903. 3. Battle of Hastings. 4. American West. 4. Mathews, Margaret Emily, 1906. 5. Chown, family name. 6. Devonshire, England. 7. Battle of West Port, Civil War. 8. Bleeding Kansas, Civil War. 9. Bourbon County, Kansas, settlers. 10. Barber County, Kansas, settlers. 11. LaJunta, Colorado, turn of 20th century. 12. Ludlow Strike.
                                                                                                I. Title

Cover illustration: This is the first known group photo of our Chown family. Pictured are William and Mary Chown and their progeny sprawled out across the prairie of either Kiowa, Kansas, or LaJunta, Colorado, sometime between 1890 and 1900.

Dedication

I have been told by my editor, Drollene Brown, to dedicate this book to somebody—someone who really inspires me to want to connect our Chown past and Chown future. Well . . . how 'bout this guy: Walter C. Chown! Which one, you ask? How 'bout both of them?

To Walter C. Chown I, my father, who made his tall tales of yesteryear so tantalizingly glorious that I always wanted to know more.

And to Walter C. Chown II, my son, who, like it or not, is one of the people most responsible for carrying the baton into the future.

I also nominate as co-dedicant (is that a word?) his sister, our daughter, Lisa Ann Dempsey. We are every bit as proud of her, our son-in-law Scott and all our "Dempsey-Chowns" as we are of our "Chown-Chowns."

Now let's tread on down the trail
Of this long and tawdry tale!

Table of Contents

Illustrations

IV. Family Years

Preface

WHAT YOU ARE ABOUT TO EMBARK UPON IS ONE MAN'S VERSION OF ONE PARTICULAR BRANCH of the Chown Family Tree . . . my branch. I am Thomas A. Chown II, born in Columbus, Ohio, on April 23, 1943, to Walter C. Chown I and Margaret Emily (Mathews) Chown. I grew up hearing my father's stories of ancestral lore, but only recently have I uncovered enough factual data to begin putting some meat on the bones of my dad's stories.

What follows is my best effort to create a flowing story line of the direct paternal path of some pretty colorful male Chown characters. As the story flowed from my pen, I realized that all these men—and their wives as well—were a tough, charismatic, optimistic and buoyant bunch. They truly represent the resilient people who made America work.

As to why knowledge of one's family history is important I offer several clichés as discussion points.

1. You must know where you've been in order to know where you're going.
2. Those who ignore history are bound to repeat it!
3. How the hell did I get here?
4. The ignorant guy who was born on third base may think he hit a triple.

In other words, whether or not we care to admit it, we are all mentally, physically, financially and in most every other way products of those who went before us. (The apple doesn't fall far from the tree.)

My Sermon

I don't intend to discuss any of these thoughts individually other than to draw a general conclusion. As I age, I think I am witnessing a troubling change in America. More and more we are obsessed with trivia, with the here and now. We have tunnel vision, seeing only our own lives, with little apparent concern as to how we came to be where we are and who made what sacrifices to get us here. I have trouble discerning any interest at all in the struggles of previous generations. The only concern seems to be what the hot topic is today and what's in it for me . . . right now! I would like to encourage, at least, my own descendants to take a broader view of humankind and to try to see themselves as one individual car on a very long train. Many cars have preceded and many will follow . . . but they are all connected, and there is a definite commonality of the paths they travel.

(End of Sermon)

When I delved into this project some years ago, I knew a paltry bit about the Chown lineage, restricted to what I had learned from my father. To proceed, I contacted a researcher in Devon,

England, who immediately provided me with wonderful documentation. Following up, I visited England to trod the cemeteries and record offices with Barbara, my sainted wife (your mother, grandmother, great-grandmother, on down the line). In England I tracked direct male lineage back to the early 1500s! This blew me away. The chart appears on the inside of the back cover.

You may note as you scan the chart that William H. Chown—we'll just call him Bill—is not only about half way between all the Roberts, Toms and Wallys, but he is also the stepping stone between the old and new worlds (England and America). His odyssey is truly dramatic, and it personifies our glance into the distant past from a fairly recent vantage point. Bill is the middle car on our train! Not only is he important due to his location on the family tree but also, as I said, he had a DRAMATIC life. That isn't to say any other Chowns along the way have been wallflowers. I'm sure even you, yourself, dear reader, are a whirlwind of excitement. Nonetheless, I offer this brief description of highlights of ol' Bill's epochal journey: born in Queen Victoria's England in 1832 . . . sailed to North America (Canada) as a child . . . was a pioneer settler in the Kansas Territory at the height of the Border War Period, 1860 . . . fought as part of the Kansas State Militia in the Civil War against rebels in an unbelievably vicious battle . . . held a homestead deed signed by Ulysses S. Grant . . . was a founding father in Kiowa, Kansas, in the 1880s . . . had first-hand experience with all the "Wild West" stuff: Indians—such as the Osage, Comanche and Kiowa—buffalo herds, wagon trains, stage coach lines, gunfighters, lynchings, great cattle drives, the Oklahoma land rush. Can any of us match that for sheer, eye-popping excitement?

Without spilling all the beans about Bill—and, yes, Mary Ellen, 'cause she was certainly there front and center as a "Pioneer Madonna" through it all—here's what I'm going to do. First I'll give you the overall, ancient Chown rundown as I have, so far, uncovered it. After that I will attempt to zero in specifically on the life of William H. Chown . . . followed by his descendants. Keep in mind I can only surmise a story line based on cold data I've gathered. However, I believe it is accurate enough to give you, dearest relative or interested friend, a decent image of the Chown path. I hope to open more windows to this saga in future years, but I'm past 60 now, and Barbara says I'm so foggy already that she wouldn't doubt if our last name eventually is proven to be Oridovich.

On the subject of accuracy, I must caution you concerning veracity when it comes to stories about (and by) our family. For example, I know my own beloved dad (Walter C. Chown I) would, on occasion, bend the truth. I want to state right now that no Chown has ever been an absolute, out-and-out liar. We have, when necessary, for the betterment of an already good story, been known to optimize the evidentiary material to suggest a preconceived conclusion. But in all other commerce or dealings with our fellowman, we shoot straight. Our word is our bond . . . e. pluribus unum . . . caveat emptor . . . and so on. Now back to the story.

Acknowledgments

I AM ALSO TOLD BY MY EDITOR THAT IN AN AUGUST LITERARY TREASURE SUCH AS THIS, A CERTAIN number of recognitions are in order. Not wanting to buck tradition—or worse yet, appear ungrateful—here is a partial list of those who helped make this volume so voluminous.

First and foremost, the fella we all have to thank for his foresight, hindsight, creativity and overall perspicacity is, of course, me. Without me, where would this terrific tome be? Nowhere, that's where.

I should also like to thank the many kind folks in the historical societies, record offices, museums, battlefield offices, ancient churches and like places who took their time to help me find some salient piece in this genealogical puzzle. Leslie Cade of the Kansas State Historical Society was great in getting me started with William Chown militia records. So was Arnold Scofield at the National Military Site in Fort Scott, Kansas.

Alice Ricke and Jean Brown in the Kiowa Historical Museum were great. The ladies in the Otero County Courthouses in Lamar and La Junta helped me find David Frank and the "Rock House." Allen and Barbara Softly, Jo and Harold Miller, Tony Eames and David Andrews all led me to so many gems in Devonshire, England.

All along the way I seemed to find some erudite, if unknown, local historian who knew just where to look for the next all-important clue. It was great fun, and they were all such nice people.

I owe some measure of thanks to my dear, long-suffering spouse, Barbara. While she may not necessarily share my passion for "diggin' up bones," at least she didn't tie my leash to a tree in our backyard and make me stay home. Actually, she has accompanied me on all the trips in our quest for forbearers. I found if I kept her well-housed, well fed and overly wined, she was a content, pleasant and, sometimes helpful, co-sleuth. After all, I'm doing all this for you folks—her grandchildren!

My most special thanks, as I hope I make clear throughout the book, goes to my dear cousin Tom Reichert. He stays at his computerized mission control up in No Man's Land, St. Cloud, Minnesota. He not only provides many crucial records and documents for our effort he also provides the most helpful commodity of all: enthusiastic encouragement. Although Tom's last name is Reichert and he is also hot on that genealogical trail, he correctly considers himself a Chown as well. He and I, as well as his siblings, Ed, Wally and Mary Alice, all equally stem from our common grandparents, Tom and Catherine Chown.

Without Tom, I never would have kept the interest level steady enough to get this far. While we both admit our efforts and conclusions are certainly not infallible, we both share the hope that all Chowns and Reicherts from our families henceforth benefit from our joint hobby.

Having thanked these people and undoubtedly inadvertently forgotten others, I'll make one other acknowledgment. Thank God for the folks who invented the computer programs that are making it possible for these long-lost records to surface. It is now possible to find stuff seemingly lost forever. I hope this book will, in my admittedly rough and untrained way, encourage family and friends to delve into their own past. We all ultimately are branches of the same family tree. And every branch is interesting in its own way.

Epigraph

This Royal Throne of Kings, this Sceptred Isle,
This earth of majesty, this seat of Mars,
This other Eden, demi-paradise,
This fortress built by Nature for herself
Against infection and the hand of war.
This happy breed of men, this little world,
This precious stone set in the silver sea,
Which serves it in the office of a wall,
Or as a moat defensive to a house,
Against the envy of less happier lands,
This blessed plot, this earth, this realm,
This England.

William Shakespeare

1

How the Chowns Came to England

Our story starts in the 11th century when William the Conqueror, that Norman butt-kicker, whom you really wouldn't want to refer to as "Bill," decided to invade England. The date was 1066 and the place was Hastings. Coincidentally, this is called the Battle of Hastings. I have in my possession several good books describing Duke William's life and rise to power. His main attributes seem to have been quick, decisive and overwhelmingly brutal treatment of his competitors. He had risen to the position of top dog in Norman France and eventually set his eyes on England. At that time, England was splintered with regard to who was most likely to be the next king. Harold Godwineson, who was probably the most capable, had marched north to meet the challenge of Norwegian King Harald Hardrada at Stamford Bridge, well north of London. Norway Harald was one giant of a man, with a great battle résumé, but Harold Godwineson got to Stamford Bridge on September 25, 1066, with "the firstest and the mostest;" he thumped big Harald and his Viking raiders. More than 300 ships had been necessary to bring the Vikings to England. Twenty-four were enough to take the survivors home. (Lots of heads, arms and legs remained behind, as fertilizer. That's why England is so green.)

When Harold Got Shot in the Eye

While at Stamford Bridge, English Harold got wind that Dangerous Duke William of Normandy had landed near Hastings on the English Channel coast; then Harold made a really big mistake. He forced his exhausted warriors to hotfoot it back at breakneck speed to meet William and his invaders—no rest for the weary. After the recent head-lopping with Norway Harald, these guys were bushed. Toting all their chain mail and battleaxes, they made it back by October 13. In addition to fatigue, the Saxons (English) were the current day equivalent of Woody Hayes (if you don't know who Woody Hayes was, you shouldn't be reading this) having a three-yards-and-a-cloud-of-dust fighting mentality. On the other hand, the Normans, under William, were much more mobile . . . with a cavalry! They had and used war horses like nothing the Saxons had ever seen. Plus, the Normans relied heavily on multitudes of archers. (Sort of the early version of the forward pass.) So while the Saxons were lined up as they had always done to fight with axes and swords, the Normans shelled 'em with arrows and then mowed 'em down with war horses. To make a long story short, Harold got shot in the eye and assumed room temperature. The Saxons were finished, and Duke William became King of England.

Guess who was with William the Conqueror? A certain Mr. Chown, that's who! I don't know exactly which Mr. Chown, but according to a family tree surname search I was gullible enough to buy, the Chown name is of Viking/Normandy origin. The search results show that Duke William took a census of most of Norman England in 1086 for the Domesday Book. Any family name in the book and dating back to Hastings is a big deal. The Chown surname, according to the book I read, "emerged as a notable English family name in the County of Kent and they were anciently seated." (While I, on the other hand, am just frequently seated.) The report goes on to say that in the following two centuries, the Chowns migrated to Sussex and as far west as Cornwall.

Fair Lawn

The report next mentions "Fair Lawn in Kent." You can read all this for yourself in any book on the Norman Invasion, and in any easy-to-buy surname research on Chown. You are welcome to read my copies, but depending on whether I'm alive or in Valhalla—get the Viking connection?—chances are your parents (my children) put all this family tree stuff right on the funeral pyre with me!

Here's what we know (or suspect) so far. The Chown name is of Norman Viking origin, its bearers having entered England in 1066 in the victorious army of William the Conqueror at the Battle of Hastings. Please do not confuse Norman with French. We are not in any way related to those rude, spineless weenies, the French! We are Norman, originally "North Men." Got it? Being north men, isn't it logical we should have moved to Florida?

Okay, we've made it to England and are at Fair Lawn in Kent. I found more information about the Chown mansion in connection with a lithograph (shown in Plate I following Chapter 2) created by J.P. Neale in October 1821. The description of the estate proves we were there!

> Fair Lawn is situated in the parish, and within half a mile of the village, of Shipborne, on the road from Wrotham to Tunbridge; from the latter town it is distant four miles. The Mansion is large, and owes its present appearance to its successive possessors. But the principal portion, which has evidently undergone many alterations, is believed to have been built about the latter end of the seventeenth century, and subsequently great additions have been made to the building. It is now a large, substantial, and convenient edifice, adorned with very extensive shrubberies, and pleasure grounds, and most excellent gardens, and seated in a finely wooded park, the smooth verdure of which may account for its name.
>
> The Estate is in Wrotham Hundred, and in Aylesford Lathe. In the early part of the reign of Edward I, it was in the possession of Adam de Barent, in whose family it remained until the latter part of the reign of Edward III. It was then transferred to the family of Colepeper, who retained possession of the Manor until early in the fourteenth century, when it became the property of the Chown family. It was sold to Sir Henry Fane of Hadlow, who died at Rouen 1596,

seized besides his Manor and Mansion at Hadlowe, &tc., of the Manors of Shipbourne, alias Shibborne, with the appurtenances; parcel of the Priory of Dartford, in Shibborne and Wroteham; of Shibborne, alias Puddenham; parcel of the Priory of Tunbridge, with the Rectory of the Chapel of Shibborne; parcel of the Priory of St. John's of Jerusalem in England, &tc. &tc., the whole of which descended to his son Sir Henry, who also purchased this Mansion of Sir George Chown. Sir Henry resumed the name of his ancestors Vane, which his posterity have since continued. [My italics for Chowns phrases.]

How do you like them apples? Don't be dismayed by the differences in spelling of place names withint those two paragraphs. Apparently spelling wasn't such a big deal back then. In fact, in the aforementioned treatise on the Chown name, there are included these various spellings: "Chowne, Chown, Chun, Chiowne, Chioune, Choon, Chiown, Cone, Chone, Cowne, Cown, Coun, Coune, Chune, Choone, Chiowne, and many more."

Now, I realize we may not be directly related to this particular Chown who lived in the 1300s, but hey, how many Chowns could have been running around back then? It's not as though we have a name like Smith or Jones, right? And here comes the good part. Barbara and I actually went there and saw it! We went to England in 2002 to track down what we could and, lo and behold, there really is a present day Fair Lawn in Shipbourne . . . in Kent. Exactly as depicted in the old lithograph, the mansion sits on gorgeous grounds surrounded by rolling hills and flocks of sheep. It's right down the road from St. Giles Church (Norman architecture) and adjacent pub.

When we buzzed at the gate we were told, "Go away. We don't allow the public in." But when I informed the caretaker we were "the Chowns, back to see our old estate . . . and all the way from Florida," he came to his senses and opened the gate! We were not allowed inside the mansion (it is now owned by a Saudi Prince), but we were shown the grounds. The caretaker turned out to be very nice and even pointed out the rear window of the room used by the Queen Mum, Queen Elizabeth's mother, who had recently died. Seeing Fair Lawn was a great experience. I just can't figure out how we let it slip out of the family. I'm not sure the caretaker believed my story, but I know there is Chown DNA on some of those doorknobs!

2

Exploring Our English Past

THE NEXT HUNDRED YEARS OR SO ARE A BIT OF A BLUR. OTHER THAN THE PREVIOUSLY-mentioned comments that "they moved far west to Cornwall," I have found no actual Chown records for that period. Nevertheless, the main purpose of our trip was to see and verify what seemed to be pretty accurate information on my direct male line of Chowns in Devonshire, on the southwest coast of England.

Devon

About a year before our trip I forced myself onto the World Wide Web and dialed up Devon, England. I took a stab at Devon only because one of the very few Chowns I have ever met told me that's where his branch hailed from. The Internet Superhighway brought me to a historical society, then to genealogy . . . and then I stumbled onto the name of an absolutely delightful couple named Jo and Harold Miller, doing family tree research under the name Devon Archive in Topsham, just below Exeter. They were invaluable. I explained to them the sum total of my knowledge: my great grandfather was William H. Chown, born in 1832, perhaps (I hoped), in Devon. (I had gotten the 1832 from his death certificate in La Junta County a couple of years earlier.) For a whopping $70, about two weeks later the Millers sent me the fairly complete list of my direct male line back to about 1540, the chart on the inside of the back cover. A much longer and detailed list is around somewhere . . . unless it was also thrown onto my funeral pyre. Well, needless to say, I was beside myself with joy, amazement and a burning desire to dedicate the rest of my life to fleshing out the truly fabulous Chown family skeleton I had been given. And Barbara fully shared my exuberance. (Okay, that may be an example of the Chown trait of slightly stretching the truth I mentioned earlier.)

Now here we were with a blueprint for investigating my great-to-the-tenth-power grandfather in a truly lovely part of England. (They say lovely a lot over there.) Fortunately, this exploration would be conducted all in the English language, with supposedly corroborating records. So off we went to Merry Olde England. In June 2002, we spent the first two weeks basically working out of Sidmouth, on the southwest coast, in Devon, trying to locate the places where my ancestors had lived . . . according to the Millers.

We stayed the first week at Hunters Moon, a very old and charming inn that had at one time in the 1800s been the Sidmouth Residence of the Anglican Bishop of Exeter and his . . .

mistress. (Ahem!) Sidmouth is an absolutely delightful seaside town dating back many, many centuries. In fact, most of the small towns we saw date back a thousand years or so. As mentioned, the Normans came aboard in the eleventh century and started moving west, but prior to their arrival, the Saxons, Romans, Druids and others all called this area home. A terrific, exhaustive book on this general area of England is Rutherford's *Sarum*, which I read prior to the trip. Sidmouth, the port town of the River Sid in the ancient Sid valley, clearly has been an important gathering spot for a long time.

According to our research, William H. (which, it happens, stands for Henry) Chown was born in Sidbury in 1832 and departed that town for Canada as an infant. And so we started our diggin' for bones in Sidbury. It might have made more sense to start in the sixteenth century and work forward, but we did the reverse. We started at the jumping off spot and went back in time. Sidbury is only five or ten miles inland up the Sid River from coastal Sidmouth. We see that William was born there in 1832, his father Robert in 1809, and his grandfather Robert in 1775. (There were five Bobs in a row.) We see that Bill's mother's name was Mary, and his grandmother's name was Jane. His father was a farmer and his grandfather an annuitant. This may mean a retired pensioner; I'm not sure. Farming was a pretty good livelihood through the early nineteenth century, due to the Napoleonic wars. Food had to be provided to soldiers and sailors in a built-up military. But when Wellington whipped Napoleon at Waterloo in 1815, it signaled the end of the good times for farmers and probably set the stage for Robert (and Mary?) to leave for the New World (Canada) with their young son, Bill, around 1834.

An indication of tough times is a petition signed by local farmers (including John and Robert Chown) asking for reestablishment of a cattle market fair in Sidbury. The charter from the year 1290 had granted it, and they wanted it back.

Sidbury

St. Giles Church was our first stop in Sidbury. We were optimistically hoping to find a Chown gravestone . . . and we did! Almost the very first one we stumbled over was "Robert R. Chown, died 1880, age 66 years . . . wife Thursa . . ." This had to be at least a second wife, and we're not even sure if this is a related Chown. But it is a Chown! Whether it's a cousin, uncle or whatever, it's a Chown. Paydirt!

St. Giles is a thousand-year old church. On the wall inside is a listing of past church wardens; among the names are Robert Chown (1810) and John Chown (1830). More paydirt! While at the church we met Lady Elizabeth Cave, the mother of the current Lord of the Manor. (Can you believe they still have lords of manors? The only manors I've ever had are bad manners!) She was pleased we came all the way from Florida to see their little town and thrilled about our success so far. But, she explained, if we really wanted to speak to the genealogy experts we must meet Barbara and Allen Softly. They were the wonderful couple who had compiled the most information and had in fact written the books on Sidbury history. Lady Elizabeth gave us directions for walking over to Bundels, the Softlys' thatched cottage. Everything in Sidbury is within a short walk of a couple of minutes.

We found Bundels and were immediately mesmerized by this adorable, picturesque, over 350-year-old cottage. Disney couldn't construct a more authentic, English-looking, thatched cottage. We knocked on the door and were at first received somewhat coolly by Mrs.

Softly. She and her husband were having lunch, she informed us, and we could come back later. When we did return an hour later, she and Mr. Softly invited us in and told us the general background of Sidbury. I bought one of her booklets on it and we left . . . a little disappointed. Yes, Chowns were here, and yes, they would have lived close by. That was about it.

To our delight, we got a call that night at Hunters Moon from Barbara Softly, who was slightly apologetic for being a bit abrupt that day. (There was certainly no need for an apology; we're the ones who had interrupted their meal.) She invited us for lunch and tea the next day, and we accepted with great enthusiasm. The second visit was terrific and very warm, and they quickly became Allen and Barbara. They gave us a total tour, upstairs and down, of the cottage, telling us that Robert Chown, annuitant, and wife, Jane (your many times great grandmother, don't forget) most likely lived in one of the several old cottages on their street . . . possibly the very one we were in! I asked what would eventually happen to Bundels. The Softlys, who have no children, said very few people would want it due to the requirement of its physical upkeep, with its extensive and breathtaking garden, and the cost of maintaining the roof thatch. To our amazement, Barbara said the locals don't have a huge passion for it . . . they're more into the "modern conveniences." For a moment I considered saying, "Well, when you and Allen get ready to sell, give me a call," but one glance from my own Barbara squelched that.

Since it will not be part of your inheritance, I will describe it for you as evocative of centuries past. And, may I add, it would help to be very short to live there. The heavily beamed 300-year-old ceilings were perfect for the average-height Englishman of yesteryear. In one room after another I had to duck my over six-foot frame—which was once six-foot three inches until termites went to work on my skeleton. Noticing I had to keep ducking, Allen asked, "My God, are all you Americans giants?"

Having earlier commented that the Robert Chowns might have lived in this exact cottage, Barbara Softly retracted her statement. Upon longer consideration, she concluded the Chowns were more likely to have lived in a nearby section of Mount Pleasant, long since torn down. Still thinking, she finally declared she could absolutely guarantee they had lived and been tenant farmers at Furzehill Farm—just up the road—in the late 1700s and possibly up to when they left in about 1834. Records show Robert and Jane and Robert's mother, Betty, lived at Furzehill. Incidentally, I'm not including all the various record copies I have in this dissertation. You can either just believe me (at your peril!) or find them in my stacks of stuff, unless it all was set ablaze on my funeral pyre. Or better yet, get off your duff and go re-create the whole project yourself. Oh, excuse me ... I'm told that on occasion I tend to be a little direct.

We asked Barbara Softly if she could point us to Furzehill Farm and make an introductory call for us to the current occupants. Yes to the former, no to the latter. Furzehill, on the site of an old Roman circle fort, was just a quarter-mile down the road and directly across the street from the old Sidbury Mill. This mill had been there forever and the Robert Chown families would most certainly have used it. But according to Barbara Softly, the current residents were two or more families she did not know. She didn't think her call would help. Disappointment! But as we were driving by Furzehill on our way out of town, we (I) decided, what the hell. The worst they could do was throw us off the property. So we (I) just parked in their drive and knocked on the door   . . . in the pouring rain.

A woman who looked to be in her sixties or seventies answered, and I blurted, "Hi, I'm

Tom Chown from America and my people lived in your house 170 to 200 years ago. Can we see it?" And I clenched my teeth awaiting her rude and caustic answer.

"Well, come on in and meet the family. Sure you can see it, and we're tickled to see you," she replied.

They couldn't have been nicer. Mrs. Porter welcomed us and introduced us to her daughter, Gail Porter, and son-in-law, Andy Wiseman. Together they had bought Furzehill Farm a couple of years earlier and were keeping as much original as possible, remodeling where necessary. Mrs. Porter went back to wake up her husband, Bernard, who appeared to be in his seventies or eighties. He had been taking a nap. (My kind of guy!) As she informed him that American past tenants of the property were in the living room, I heard him remark with concern, "My God, they haven't come to claim the house, have they?"

As we had tea in front of the old fireplace, which was more than 200 years old, I just couldn't soak it all in. To think, my great grandfather William (little Billy?) probably sat in front of this fire as an infant, as his father, Robert, and grandfather Robert looked on. I know my wife, Barbara, was almost moved to tears of joy! (Ahem.) We spent the remainder of the day at Furzehill. Andy and Gail took us through the old long barn, which ran parallel with and right along the road. The original cob wall, a clay and straw mix, is still there; the old beams are easily two-foot square. As before, everything I saw seemed to have Chown written all over it (especially the slight whiff of ancient horse manure).

One other fun and interesting experience in Sidbury was lunch at the Red Lion Inn. We stopped into the pub for lunch and a pint only because it was right across the street from the Sidbury Church. In further reading we discovered all these old churches had a pub across the street that were a part of the church property from earliest times. Since the workers who built the church and eventually the congregation itself were centered there, they needed a meeting place for food and drink. Thus, a pub. The day we were there, England was playing Argentina, I think, in a World Cup Soccer match; everyone was glued to the TV. (These people have no idea what real football is!) We could have walked out with all the furniture and nobody would have noticed. I gently ribbed them about their sissified version of "football," and they gently asked why we claimed "World Champs" in games like American football, baseball and basketball that are basically only played in America. I left a very small tip, and we left.

Ottery St. Mary

On we went, back in time, to Ottery St. Mary. As you can see in the Chown direct male list, Robert Chown and aforementioned wife, Betty, lived in Ottery St. Mary. He was born in 1754, and they married in 1774. Although we did not uncover any Chown presence in Ottery, we enjoyed the day. The drive over from Sidbury in our rental Chrysler PT Cruiser was great. We took the back way out of Sidbury, which meant we were driving on extremely tight "hedgerow" roads. These roads, more like pathways, date way back before any notion of cars. The hedgerows are centuries old, many feet thick and often six or more feet high. The effect can be like driving in a tunnel. Should you meet another vehicle (we normally didn't), somebody has to back up. In addition, as you know, they drive on the wrong side of the road from the wrong side of the car! (I pointed this out to some of the locals, but they don't take constructive criticism well.)

Ottery St. Mary Church is a gorgeous, smaller replica of Exeter Cathedral. We toured it, saw the list of their vicars dating back to the twelfth century, found no Chowns, and adjourned to the London Inn, the local pub. Normally we don't drink a lot, but something about the overwhelming sentiment and emotion of all this Chown bone-hunting was driving us both to drink! I could tell all these pints of beer were just adding to the almost delirious joy Barbara was already experiencing ... (Ahem!)

Rockbeare

We were really getting into the distant past now. Rockbeare is a very little, very old town located about half-way between Ottery St. Mary and Exeter. Our list showed that four of our Chowns were born and lived in this extremely picturesque, tiny hamlet. There were two more Roberts (born 1729 and 1690), a Charles (1648) and a George (1628). You can see their wives' names on the descendant list, so I won't repeat them. This place probably moved me more than anything we saw. The old church is lovingly looked after by David Andrews, church warden. It is not open to the public, per se, due to its age and fragility, I'm sure. But it is stunning. Before meeting with Dave, we entered the church grounds and adjoining cemetery.

The moment we stepped off the sidewalk—Barbara was leading due to her unbridled enthusiasm and passion for perusing graveyards—she jumped back and exclaimed, "Whoa! Hold up! You're not going to believe this!"

And there they were. The very first two tombstones, covered in moss and lichens and almost unreadable, were for Edmund Chown and Elizabeth Chown! All told, we found about a half-dozen Chowns, most of them having died in the mid-nineteenth century. Now keep in mind I don't have the foggiest idea who these people were. I don't think any were "direct" family, but I'm sure they were all related to us. Great aunts, uncles, cousins . . . whatever. I'm sure a lot of the old, old trees in that graveyard have Chown DNA in their branches. Another fact to keep in mind is that the beginning of our direct lineage in England predates the graves in Rockbeare. Moreover, any graves prior to the 1800s probably don't have stones, principally because deterioration has finished them off. We saw plenty more stones that were either totally unreadable or totally crumbled, some of which were probably "our" Chowns. A second reason for our not finding older stones is that back in the 1400-1700 period, ordinary people were not given a stone marker. The important church people were buried under the floor in the church. The rest of the commoners were buried "wherever" and with a wood marker that didn't last. Nonetheless, just seeing the name Chown on some stones in that medieval churchyard was an experience.

We then met David Andrews, who escorted us into the church itself and explained its history. The ancient Norman architecture, windows and crowned kings' and queens' heads on the outside are really eerie. David explained that the inside's being in two halves is due to an ancient fire; this is, roughly, a thousand-year-old church. Wow! We made a small donation (but much larger than our tip back at the Red Lion Pub) to David for help with church maintenance. If I could (and you should, too), I would send some token amount to these old churches now and then—purely from a sentimental and historical viewpoint. I would absolutely hate for them to ever just decay off the face of the earth. Most of the Chown habitats were wood or cob and thatch and have long ago rotted away. To stand in these churches and graveyards and ancient villages and realize a part of us was here . . . to me is very moving. Much more important, to reiterate, a big reason we are where we are and who we are today is because of who and where they were a hundred, two hundred and five hundred years ago. I implore you, you future Chowns, to some day go to Rockbeare and stand in that churchyard and know that what you are feeling is what I felt back in 2002.

(And to you, dear wife of that future Chown . . . hang in there. The Jack in the Green Inn awaits you on the main road out of Rockbeare! Keep in mind, another pub, another pint. This ordeal will all be over soon!)

FAIR LAWN: Then and Now

PLATE 1. FAIR LAWN THEN AND NOW.

Top: 1821 engraving of Fair Lawn, by T. Matthews.

Center: Tom and Barbara Chown in the center of Fair Lawn's porticos in 2002.

Bottom: Photo of Fair Lawn taken by the author in 2002.

PLATE 2. SIDMOUTH AND ST. GILES CHURCH.

Top: Sidmouth, on the English Channel, the beautiful beach town located at the mouth of the Sid River in East Devon.

Bottom: Tom stands by the first Chown tombstone he and Barbara found, located at St. Giles Church in Sidbury, East Devon.

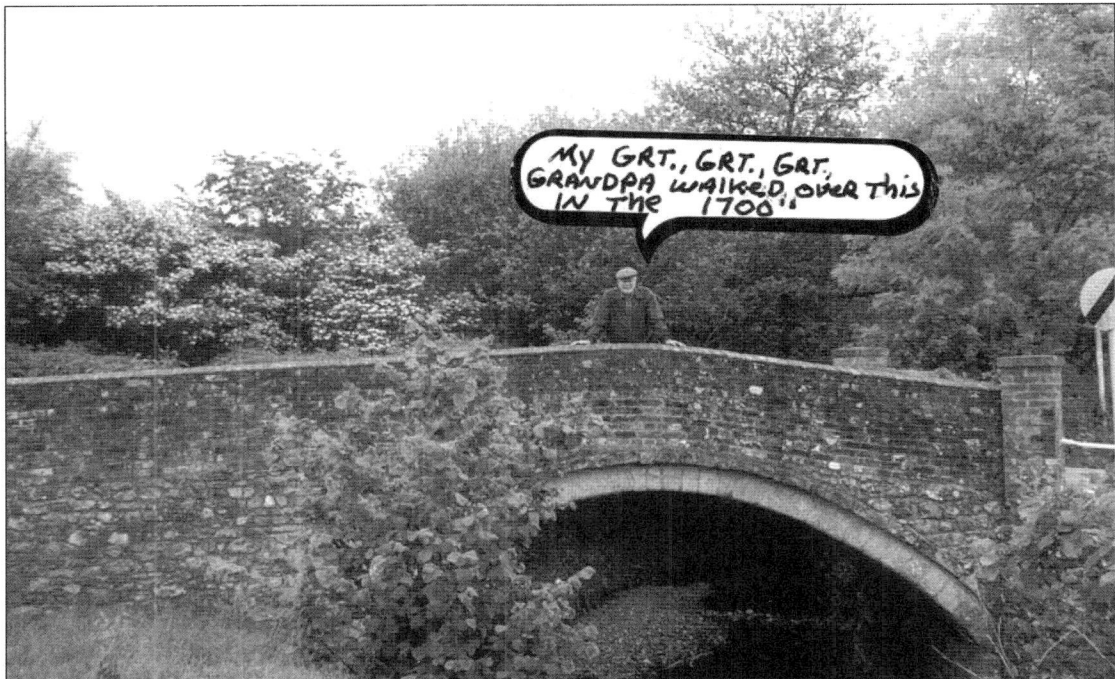

PLATE 3. SIDBURY CHURCH AND SID RIVER.

Top: Tom points out the two Chowns listed as church wardens at the Sidbury Church in the 1800s.

Bottom: Tom feels the presence of history as looks out across a bridge in Sidbury over the Sid River.

Bundels Cottage

Plate 4. Bundels Cottage.

Picturesque English cottages have names. Allen and Barbara Softly stand outside their "Bundels" in Sidbury, East Devon, surrounded by lavish, colorful flowers.

PLATE 5. ANCIENT FURZEHILL FARM.

Top: Barbara and Tom smile in front of the fireplace where the Robert Chown family enjoyed warmth from the late 1700s to about 1834.

Center: Tom believes the early Chowns must have stooped over a lot; his head hits an ancient, low beam.

Bottom: The Robert Chown family, including infant William, lived here immediately before their departure to the New World, c. 1834.

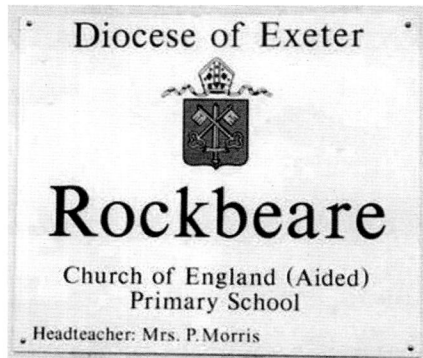

PLATE 6. ROCKBEARE CHURCH.
Tom and Barbara Chown traveled back in time to Rockbeare, Devon. Above is Rockbeare Church, a stunning ancient Norman church . . . full of Chown graves.

Top: Diocese of Exeter identification plaque.

PLATE 7. ROCKBEARE CHURCH CEMETERY.

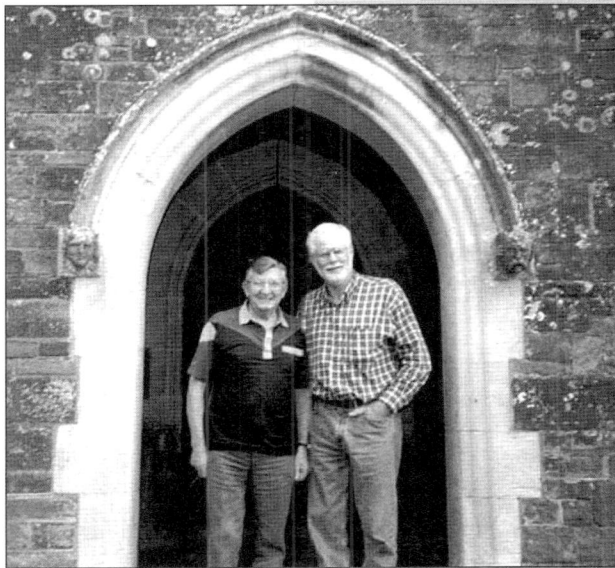

Top: Barbara finds another Chown marker.

Center: Tom with David Andrews, church warden and historian at St. Mary and St. Andrew Church in Rockbeare, Devon.

Bottom: Tom with two Chown gravestones in Rockbeare Church Cemetery.

PLATE 8. TOPSHAM, DEVON.

Top: Barbara stands in front of the Globe Hotel, a fixture in Topsham for many centuries. Tom and Barbara slept here.

Center: Tom had to sleep on the floor because he was too long for the bed.

Bottom: Tom's god-sent researchers and friends, Jo and Harold Miller.

EXETER CATHEDRAL

DEVON STUDIES CENTER

PLATE 9. EXETER CATHEDRAL (top) AND DEVON STUDIES CENTRE.

19

PLATE 10. PLYMTREE
CHURCH.

Inset at top: Tom Chown
in 2002 with the parish
record book showing the
record of Michael and
Tamsen's marriage. Wow!

Center: Plymtree Church,
the site of the marriage
of Michael and Tamsen
Chown in 1569.

Left: Anne Eames
showing Barbara the old
church keys in Plymtree,
Devon.

INSIDE OLD PLYMTREE CHURCH

PLATE 11. INTRICATE
WOOD CARVING IN OLD
PLYMTREE CHURCH.

Right: Tony Eames,
author of *The Book of
Plymtree*, points out
details in the church
rood screen.

Below: The interior of
the church shows the
rich scale of the
building's painstaking
detail work.

PLATE 12. CHOWNS POOL FARM, PLYMTREE. This farm and the building above are described in Tony Eames' *The Book of Plymtree*. Jovial Mike Jarvis, the current owner of Chowns Pool Farm, points to the place where a section of the original cob wall was taken out for Tom. The farm has been in Jarvis' family for a hundred years. Center inset: Sign on the building, which can be see just beneath the roof line in the top photo.

3

Our Summer Vacation 2002

I HAVE BECOME AWARE THAT MY NARRATIVE ABOUT CHOWN HISTORY IN ENGLAND HAS BECOME a travelogue of our trip. I guess that's a necessity, because that's how we learned it ourselves. By repeating to you what we heard, saw and thought we understood by being there is, I hope, added value to merely dry research. I certainly came away with a more authentic feel for the past by experiencing the sights, smells, topography, weather and other elements of Devon Countryside—albeit centuries later. So if this has turned into a "What we did on our 2002 summer vacation," so be it. I'll take a brief hiatus from the genealogy and give you a true travelogue on our side trip into Topsham and Exeter.

Topsham and Exeter

As I mentioned, we got a real head start on the record trail we needed from Jo and Harold Miller. The Devon Archives office indicated on their letterhead, Hope Cottage at 3 White Street in Topsham, is actually their home. It is a delightful hole-in-the-wall off an alley in this extremely old town on the Exe River. The further I got involved with the Millers by e-mail on our Chown search, the more I liked them. We developed such a sharp repartee of witty communication I assume they liked me, too. Not only did I greatly appreciate the fascinating trail of my family's past they quickly provided, I loved their humor. When I announced that we were coming over, they insisted we stop and meet them in person. We had intended to take them to lunch, but the day we arrived, Harold had done up a terrific fish meal for us, and Jo kept our wine glasses full. Oh, well, at least it was a brief departure from beer. We "pinched the purple" pretty well and really enjoyed being with the Millers.

Topsham predates Exeter and is 700 or more years old. It is right on the Exe River, and the tide is severe. We stayed at the old Globe Hotel—very atmospheric but, again, those old Limeys were too damned short. I couldn't fit in the antique bed (even though I am an antique) and had to sleep on the floor! Topsham is a really cute little town and is a good bedroom choice for seeing Exeter. With its neat shops, it is itself quite pleasant for street strolling. (We bought a black and white Devon ceramic cow there.) From Topsham it is an easy half-hour bus ride into downtown Exeter, which beats fighting traffic and searching for parking.

The Millers gave us a conglomeration of Chown references from the Exeter Flying Post, a newspaper from the 1700-1800s. Not only do these references indicate that Chowns were all over Devon, but they also give a good overview of the high lofty nature of the general

Chown character. Nowhere is the word "murderer" or even "horse thief" used, but the words "defendant," "bankrupt," "fined," and "embezzler" do appear. The notes on these discoveries are in our photo album of this trip. Read 'em and weep! (This "travelogue" pretty well follows the photo album and you can look at the photos as you read . . . unless the album was on the pyre.)

Exeter is really something. I said Topsham predates Exeter, which really isn't true. Topsham predates Exeter as a river town, but not as a town. A canal was dug way back when, extending the navigability of the Exe from Topsham on to Exeter, thereby enhancing Exeter's power as a commerce center. But Exeter goes back to Roman days in 350 A.D.—long before the river was brought to it—so it is more than 1600 years old. It sits in the middle of the West Country and most certainly has been at the cross roads of human activity there from the earliest mists of time. The most outstanding thing in Exeter is the cathedral. It is so outstanding the Nazis went out of their way to bomb it in World War II, just for spite. They damaged the cathedral but did not destroy it. It is still there, and it is magnificent. I think it dwarfs New York's St. Patrick's Cathedral. If it does not, there can be no question that the Exeter Cathedral is huge. We hooked up with a guide who really helped. He pointed out all the nook-and-cranny facts. The statues on the outside and the wood work, windows, ceilings and tombs on the inside are . . . well, just go see it!

The most important, or germane, part of our Exeter sojourn was the Devon records office. Not that I didn't trust the Millers' documentation, but I wanted to go to the Studies Center Record Room and try to double check. Barbara could hardly wait. She had been complaining that we had blown a couple of days going through shops, galleries and gardens and overeating in fine restaurants. She had a strong hunger to get into that record office and spend a day or two poring over microfiche and parish records—anything it took to see one more Chown official artifact. So I went along with her. (Since you cannot see the expression on my face as I write this, perhaps I should tell you that the foregoing is not Chown embellishment . . . it is falsehood, pure and simple.)

Getting to the office about ten minutes before it opened, we waited by the doors with eight or ten other people. One of them, hearing our Yankee accents, asked what we were up to. When we explained we were trying to research my (your) Devon ancestry back to the 1500s, they were impressed. As elsewhere—in fact, everywhere we went—when they found we had come all the way from Florida they had comments. Wherever we went in West Country, we rarely saw another American . . . or any foreigner, for that matter. All the foreign visitors go to London . . . and, perhaps on to Stonehenge or Bath . . . but seldom Devon. That, in fact, is what we really liked about it. (I'd have hated to get there and be seated in a pub right beside our next door neighbors.) Conversely, the English we talked to had all been to Disney World, New York and California. None to Venice or Dunnellon, Florida, or Ohio or Pascagoula. As the doors opened, our new acquaintances wished us good luck and hurried to their separate research areas.

The process of library research on computer, microfiche or parish books takes a certain knowhow. I've had reasonably good luck playing real dumb and getting the librarian or another library patron to help me. The underlying source of my ability to pull this off is that I am real dumb. But that's wearing thin. More and more I find you can get brief pointers, but the folks see through the "I'm too dumb to do this" routine and you have to muddle through it yourself

From Vikings to Venetians 25

(unless your devoted wife still falls for it). So there we were, Barbara and I, with copies of a few records . . . but still far from all of the male Chowns that came between William H., born 1832, and Michael, born in the 1520s. Starting at William in Sidbury, the first several going back into the 1700s were fairly easy to find. All those Roberts popped up with no great difficulty. However, by the time we got back to the last Bob and then Charles and George, things got tough. We were pretty much strictly into church records. Not only were the pages in a state of deterioration, but the writing we were trying to decipher was in "olde" English. How the hell these bishops 300-500 years ago expected a Florida Cracker (or Ohio Buckeye) to read this gibberish in the twenty-first century is beyond me.

There we were, it was 4:48 p.m. and the place was supposed to close at 5:00 p.m. We were the only two patrons left, and the librarian was straightening up to close. She approached, asking, "Have you found everything you wanted?"

With my face and voice full of dejection, I replied, "All but the most important thing I came for . . . all the way from Florida." Wondering if it were possible for me to conjure a tear in the corner of my eye and work that old Chown I'm-helpless magic, I continued, "We've found almost all the way back to the furthest-back direct-ancestor we're aware of—Michael, in Plymtree. But we haven't been able to find him. That would have been in the 1540s or so."

I stood stock still and looked at her. She looked at me, then at her watch, then at Barbara, who wanted to leave as much as the librarian did. There it was! I felt the tear well up.

"Well, we're not supposed to stay past five, but since you've come all the way from Florida, and I can see your wife is really into this too"—she glanced again at Barb, who had tears in her eyes, too!—"I guess I can see if we can help."

Yes! Not only was I elated that my I'm-dumber-than-a-post gig was still effective, but this gal might actually find our missing links. I decided not to show her the printout of the report I had gotten from the Millers, although I probably wouldn't have known I was missing something without it.

She went back to the sacrosanct dungeon and emerged several minutes later with a couple of booklets. They looked really old and weather-beaten, as though they were Shakespeare's crib notes. What they actually were was the original bishops' records from Exeter Parish (Plymtree) in the early mid-sixteenth century—not copies . . . the real books. She went whipping through them page by page the way I whip through the sports pages.

I laughed. "What are you trying to do, zinging through that fast?" I asked, seeing that every page was blotched and faded, and the writing was in old English. "Nobody can read that stuff, even with a magnifying glass."

"I can," she retorted and asked, "Did Michael marry Tamsen?"

"Well, yes he did," I answered, "but how did you know that?"

I wondered if she somehow had x-ray vision and could see the printout I had with my papers.

"Because there it is, right there."

"Right where?" I asked, staring at her pointed finger on the blackened, scribbled, fishing line-looking mess at the bottom of the page.

"Right there, can't you see it?" She read the line: "Michael Chowne and Tamsen Adames the twenty-first day of July."

This was on the page for the year 1569 in the bishop's transcripts. If Michael was, say, 23 when married, he was born in 1546. Tamsen is mentioned as "Thomasine" in the printout we got from the Millers, as well as in The Book of Plymtree, by Tony Eames. Tamsen must be a shortened version. All these record copies are in a separate black booklet I assembled. You can probably still find them unless . . . well, you know.

As far as I was concerned, this haul at the Devon Record Office alone made the trip worthwhile. I must add that, all kidding aside, the ladies at the Devon Record Office were truly invaluable. They were curteous, helpful and quite enthusiastic about our research success. Barbara wanted to hide behind a bookcase until everyone left, then search for more records by candle light. But I said no. I insisted we go clean up and proceed to the Globe's pub for a pint, a nice dinner . . . and maybe another pint! We packed it in and headed back to the Globe Hotel, and after dinner . . . a night in that midget's bed!

Plymtree

Now we get to the furthest back spot in our provable family history that we'll probably ever reach: Plymtree! This little, extremely out-of-the-way hamlet is about 30 or 40 miles northeast of Exeter. One doesn't just happen by it; it's on the way to nothing. You go there only on purpose, and we did. It's a one-street village and, as in all these villages, the most imposing structure is the church. All these date back to the same year of 1000, plus or minus a few. They are all Norman architecture, and all have the same type of clock mounted on the main tower, installed sometime after the English invented time. (I am sure if I had been around back then I would have been the commission salesman peddling those clocks!)

The Millers had given us the name of Tony Eames as Plymtree's local historian. He is the author of the book mentioned above, The Book of Plymtree. Of the very few businesses in Plymtree, I spotted a small general store with a post office sign on it. Figuring someone there might know this old Eames geezer, I inquired inside. The proprietor said he did know Mr. Eames and asked my family name.

"Chown," I replied.

Came the reply, "Hmmm . . . Chown! That's interesting. Tony Eames lives across the street. He has written an exhaustive history of Plymtree. It's a beautiful, accurate hard back with our total story back to the 1500s . . . and you are in it!"

I nearly fainted. Barb surely would have if she had not been out in the car doing her nails.

"Sure," he continued. "Your people owned and worked Chowns Pool Farm, just out of town, several centuries ago. It's not only in Eames' book . . . the farm is still there . . . sign and all."

Be still my beating heart! To me, this was like hearing a scientist decipher the pyramid hieroglyphics and declaring the name Chown was included in them. "You've got to be kidding!" I blurted.

"Nope," he declared. "Tony and Anne are home now. Go on over and see them."

When I went to the car to rouse Barbara, I knew she'd jump at the chance for another octogenarian interview. Over we went, up through a very attractive garden with a Beemer in the driveway. Our knock was answered by a rather dapper guy with salt and pepper hair and neatly trimmed mustache—Tony Eames, who was my age or younger! No old codger, he! Tony had been a barrister (lawyer) in London. Tiring of the rat race several years earlier, he and his wife had purchased this old, old home and refurbished it beautifully, without diminishing its character. In researching the history of his house, he coincidentally uncovered the story of all of Plymtree. He had so much collected data, including pictures and personal histories, he figured he might as well create a book.

Here's what he wrote about Chowns Pool Farm:

> We do not know who gave his name to Chownes tenement, the earliest reference being in 1613 when Thomasine Chowne, widow of Michael, paid church rates on some land. She died in about 1637, and her son Michael took over her land, and also White's tenement: he and his brother Robert each paid Rates on separate farms, but by 1678 Robert Land owned Michael's property as part of Woodbeer Court farm. (Robert Chown's land was also called Chownes, but when Philip Yeo purchased it in 1679 it became known as Yeo's tenement.) In 1707 Chowne's was absorbed into Charles Harward's Hayne estate, with John Godfrey as the farmer, but it became a separate holding again in 1732.

> The purchaser of Chowns Pool, as it was henceforth known, was Charles Chichester, Esq., of the well-known North Devon family, and his name appeared as the ratepayer for the next 62 years. From apprenticeship records we know the tenant farmers at various times during his ownership: Henry Bluet and his wife Mary in 1741; Henry Hatchwell in 1763; Thomas Crago in 1776; and Charles Reynolds (an Exeter weaver) in 1786. In April 1796 an advertisement appeared in the 'Exeter Flying Post': "Freehold of Chowns Pool Farm for sale. Small Farmhouse and outhouses, with 32 acres of arable, meadow, pasture & orchards. Let for the next 4 years to Thomas Crago, at £14 per Annum."

> John Shiles, who for some time had farmed a small tenement called Sock as well as farming Woodbeer Court for Elizabeth Young, and had regularly served in various Parish offices, became the ratepayer for Chowns Pool in 1798, and was still recorded as such in 1835. He died in that year, to be succeeded at both farms by his younger brother, Henry.

> The Tithe Apportionment of 1842 showed that Henry Shiles' own farm consisted of 32½ acres, but the 202½ acres of Woodbeer Court must have taken up most of his time.

The day I met Tony, of course, I had not read that entry, but I knew I wanted to buy a book. When I asked to buy a copy, I was disappointed to hear that Tony had sold them all. The day was saved by one of Tony's neighbors, who was kind enough to sell me his copy, saying he would eventually find another. These Plymtree people were wonderfully gracious!

The Plymtree church, or at least the ground it sits on, has been the town's meeting place for a long time. Tony gave us a very thorough tour. His lovely wife Anne took us over and unlocked the doors with what looked like the original keys to the kingdom. Tony stayed back at the house for thirty minutes to print out all the mentions of Chown in the Plymtree records—baptisms, marriages, burials and such. Below is a copy of what he pulled from the Internet:

CHOWN families at PLYMTREE, East Devon
Baptisms:
Chowne, John, s. of Michael - 3 Oct. 1570
Chowne, Agnes, d. of Michael - 8 May 1572
Chowne, Augustine, s. of Michael - 7 Aug. 1574
Chowne, Mellony, d. of Michael - 16 Mar. 1576/7
Chowne, William, s. of Michael - 19 Jan. 1579/80
Chowne, Syth, d. of Michael - 14 July 1582
Chowne, Robert, s. of Michael - 28 Nov. 1584
Chowne, Elizabeth, d. of Michael - 28 Apr. 1587
Chowne, Richord, d. of Michael - 23 Oct. 1628
Chowne, Austen, s. of Michael - 17 Apr. 1631
Chowne, Elizabeth, d. of Michael - 4 Sep. 1632
Chowne, John, s. of Michael - 4 Sep. 1634
Chowne, Robert, s. of Robert - 5 Oct. 1636

Marriages:
Chowne, Michael & Tamsen Adames - 21 July 1569
Hacke, Thomas & Sith Chowne [BTs only] - 15 Sep. 1606
Chowne, Robert & Joan Horne - 20 Feb. 1609/10
Broadmeade, Richard & Elizabeth Chowne - 15 Sep. 1617

Burials:
Chowne, Michael - 13 Jun. 1611
Chowne, Agnes, w. Of Michael - 20 Sep. 1658

The Devon Subsidy [tax] of 1624
Thomasine Crowne [sic]

Apprentice Indentures
21.6.1779: Sarah Hollings apprenticed to Robert Gould for
    Deans Mill - Witness: Edmund Choun

Churchwardens' accounts:
1613: Widow Choune paid 20d. Rate for church repairs.
1616: Robert Choun was Churchwarden [his account does
    not survive].
1618: Widow Chowne paid 4s.-6d Rate for repairing the
    church. [The rate for a house was 3d.]
1620-23: Widow Chowne paid church Rates of 1s.-6d.
1624-25: Thomasine Chowne paid Church Rates of 6s.
1626-27: Thomasine Chowne paid Church Rates of 2s.-3d.
c. 1628: Robert Chowne was Churchwarden [his account
    does not survive].
1630: Thomasine Chowne paid 3s. Rates
1632: Michael Chowne was Churchwarden
1634: Michael Chowne paid 2s. Rates, & Thomasine 2s.-3d
1634: Michael Choune [sic] paid 2s.-3d. "For his mother's
    tenement" & 3s.-8d "for Whites"
1636: Michael & 'widow' Chowne paid Rates

1638 Michael Chowne paid 1s.-3d. & Robert Chowne paid
    rates for their tnenments.
1650-1655: Michael Chowne & Robert Chowne paid Rates
    for their tnenments.
1656: Record of money paid for charitable uses:
    "ffrom Richard Chowne of Taunton but not as yet payd
    to mee - one pound"

1868: Henry Chown owed 8s.-5½ d. Church Rate arrears for
    his property.

As I glanced at the paper later, I saw that, sure enough, my eleven times grandfather, Michael, and his wife, Tamsen Adams, are listed with their twelve children. Tamsen is listed as "Thomasine Chowne," "widow Chowne" and just plain "Chowne." No matter, it is she! My fondest dream is for some future Chown to have a baby girl, name her Thomasine and call her Tamsen. No pressure, of course!

Like the other churches we had seen, the church at Plymtree was fascinating, especially in a one-on-one tour guided by Tony Eames. He was clearly passionate about preserving the structure and its history. I, like the Softlys in Sidbury, lament the general lack of interest and financial support these old churches get in remote England. (As I thought about it, I was reminded of the concern, or lack thereof, we are giving our Revolutionary and Civil War sites in the USA.) Tony pointed out the 1,100-year-old yew tree beside the church. From ancient times, yew trees were planted to serve as meeting locations. By Henry VIII's time (just before Michael and Tamsen were born), weekly archery practice was mandatory for all local men at the yew tree. The wood from these trees made good arrows. The church, the tree and the meeting of the home guard apparently all melded in this tradition.

From Tony's explanation, I could almost see old Michael (and his father, Robert, I think) plus some of Michael's sons—John, Augustine, William, Robert, Austen—flinging arrows around. And over there, under the branches of that already huge yew tree, those good-looking daughters—well, come on now . . . you cannot doubt they were all good looking!—are serving up corn dogs and fritters and ice cold Coronas! When you include sons and daughters-in-law, you see that Michael and Tamsen produced a regular Plymtree plethora all by themselves! And that's a damn good thing for you and me, right?

We hated to leave that church yard. I felt ghosts everywhere. No Chown grave markers, though, because the Chown presence there predated by far any lasting grave stones. But the Chowns had been there . . . yessir, we were there!

On our way out of town, we planned to look for Chowns Pool Farm.

Chowns Pool Farm

For the past hundred years or so, Chowns Pool Farm has been owned by the Jarvis Family. When we were there the owner was Mike Jarvis—and before him, his father and grandfather. I almost woke Mike up when I knocked on the door at three p.m.; he was just getting up. The reason is a sad one. Not only does Mike's wife work in an office while he works the farm, but also, due to hard times, he has a second job driving a truck to London and back every night.

Mad Cow Disease, and Milk Disease before that, have really hurt farmers in Devonshire, a big dairy cow area. Mike is barely holding on, but he's a cheerful guy! When I realized I might have awakened him, I apologized profusely.

"Nonsense," he said, and then fell all over himself being friendly. We hit it off immediately. Good or bad times, Mike—who has a totally engaging personality—is a roly-poly guy who looks like a man who has never missed a pork chop. "Well I'll be damned," he exclaimed when I told him I was a Chown. "This place has always had that Chowns Pool sign out there, and we never had any idea where it came from or who the Chowns were." (He apparently hadn't read Tony Eames' book.) He shook his head. "And here I am looking at a real, live Chown!"

He showed me around the fields—twenty-five or fifty acres—and then said he wanted to show me something. We walked over to the original long barn at the road. Leading me inside, he pointed at the far wall, where old cob (mud/straw) was falling in, but still there. "As far as I know, that's the original wall," he stated, "and your ol' Chowns probably laid it up."

Wow! Here I was with the same reverential willies I had experienced at Furzehill Farm, in the Rockbeare church graveyard and at the Plymtree church yew tree. I was now similarly awed in the 400- to 500-year-old long barn of Chowns Pool Farm!

I don't know why this moves me so. I certainly realize all this historiatin' won't put food on the table today, and nobody really seems to care. But I care! Yessir, I care. Right now, in the year of our Lord 2004, I count as great blessings my wonderful wife, Barbara, our two grown children, Walter C. Chown II and Lisa A. (Chown) Dempsey, our son-in-law, Scott Dempsey and our five granchillun: Michael, Megan, Kate, Tac (Thomas A. Chown III) and Mary Mac. Of course that means our Chown blood will keep flowing on down to . . . you! Now keep in mind there's no exclusivity or snobbishness intended in this. I, myself, in addition to Chown blood, have the blood of Rodden, McGinnis and all those maiden names that have gone before. Barbara is a Bain and a Massenelli. Throw in such names as Dempsey, Browning, McGriff and many others, and you can see that we all stem from hundreds, thousands, perhaps millions of family branches . . . back to Adam and Eve if you lean that way. My point is this: I got a great feeling of connection—or maybe a better word is belonging—to something much bigger than myself as I stood in that long barn.

I asked Mike if he would permit me to chip off a small piece of the cob as a memento. He cheerfully agreed, and we chunked off a tennis ball-size piece and put it in a plastic bag. He suggested we put in a little water to keep it moist, otherwise it would crumble. Oddly enough, this small ancient morsel has a faint odor suggesting maybe the original mud had a type of organic material imbedded in it commonly found in barn yards containing cows. It really lends credibility to the story, since most Chowns have been full of that substance ever since!

Every time I stumbled onto one of these ancient Chown "shrines," I wanted to buy it. Wouldn't it be neat to go back several centuries later and buy Chowns Pool Farm, in the beautiful, quiet, pastoral Devon countryside. I have only three things stopping me. One: no money. Two: your great grandmother Barbara would leave me, thus lousing up this whole warm, cuddly story. And three: what the hell would I (we . . . you) do with it? But those places sure are fun to visit. Just ask Barbara.

End of England

To sum up, let's rehash this quickly in its chronological direction. We now have at least a reasonably accurate handle on the Chown journey.

At some prehistoric point, our caveman ancestor, Muchowngup, morphed into Chown the Viking. He and his ilk marauded through the North Sea, stopping only to plunder, pillage, drink, fight and ravish the women. (I'm trying to find something to criticize here!) Eventually they stormed into northwestern France, that part bordering the English Channel.

The French King hustled on down and said "Look, I know all about you ill-mannered Vikings . . . you Northmen . . . especially Chown, there. We can't have you mixing with us blue-blooded French around Pareé, so here's the deal. You stay over here and we'll actually give you this area. You can even call it Nor-man-dy, after yourselves if you want. Or Slobenia after Chown, if necessary . . . whatever. But to consummate this fine offer you must agree to three demands. One, do not inflict your insufferable ways on us. We're too delicate for that. And for God's sake stay down wind of us. Two, we encourage you to keep your murderous, plundering appetites intact, just aim them at England. And three, you are absolutely forbidden to ever, by design or drunken disorder, allow any Chown bloodline to mix into our oh-so-pure French pedigree."

(To the best of my knowledge such interaction has never happened. I have reason to believe we have on occasion been attracted to sheep, but thank God, never the French.)

And that brings us back to Duke William and The Battle of Hastings in 1066 . . . the Domesday Book in 1086 . . . Fair Lawne in the 14th Century . . . and then 300 years or so livin' the good life in Devon. We somehow, as described, settled in Plymtree in the 1500-1600s, then on to Rockbeare, Ottery St. Mary and Sidbury through the 16-, 17- and 1800s . . . until about 1834.

4

The Big Leap . . . And Beyond

I'M NOT GOING TO GO INTO ANY MORE DETAIL ABOUT WILLIAM H. CHOWN AT THIS POINT beyond any of the preceding story line of Chown progress. I will merely continue the saga by pointing out the most obvious fissure in our lineage: Bye-bye, Old World, hello, New World.

I asked Allen and Barbara Softly the big "Why" question. After centuries of making their home in Devon, with much family all over, benign weather, great farm land, beautiful countryside, the seashore nearby, I can't imagine why anyone would want to leave. This was especially so when the trip entailed an absolutely killer voyage that farm people weren't used to, their destination an unknown country for an unknown life.

"Was it religious or political motivation?" I asked.

"Oh, heavens no," said Mrs. Softly. "The pilgrims and Plymouth (also in Devon) people certainly left for religious freedom, back in the 1600-1700s. But by the time your people left in 1833 or so, two problems existed. The step-down in military manpower occasioned by Waterloo became a 'Waterloo' for the farmers. With a much smaller army and navy needing to be fed and outfitted, farmers lost a lot of their market. A second reason was the custom of primogeniture, in which the eldest son always inherited the farm. Subsequent sons had nothing to fall back on, especially with a smaller farm-goods market. Thus, on to America or Australia."

I still don't know which boat Robert and Mary Chown and infant son William came over on. It very well could have been the General Wolfe. We think they emigrated in 1833 or 1834. We have in our possession a highly informative narrative written by one W.F. Chown in 1941 called "The Descendants of Roger C. and Sara T." It states:

> On April 1, 1832, Roger [Robert's brother] and Sara Chown and
> their five sons and one daughter left Seaton for Plymouth to take ship
> for Quebec. Provisions for the voyage were obtained at Plymouth and
> the family embarked on the sailing vessel General Wolfe. Five weeks
> and four days after they arrived in Quebec . . .

I guess Roger would be my three-times great uncle. If he and Sara made a successful voyage to Canada in 1832, and his brother Robert and family decided to follow a year or so later, it seems reasonable they may also have been on the General Wolfe, a ship named after British General James Wolfe—"conqueror of Quebec" in the battle of Abraham Plains, September 13, 1759, in the French and Indian War. I've tried, to no avail so far, to locate a ship's passenger list to determine exactly when, from where, and on which ship our direct ancestors Robert, Mary and little Will sailed. What a voyage it must have been! I can close my eyes and almost see them barfing their way across the Atlantic for five weeks.

My cousin Tom Reichert, of St. Cloud, Minnesota, has been instrumental in uncovering this Canadian leg of our journey. Both Tom and I have proven to be passionate about unlocking the mysteries of our common Chown ancestry. Our common grandfather, Thomas Albert Chown I (1876, Kansas . . . see the Rodden family tree booklet by Meg Kalmerton), had two children. They were Walter C. Chown I, my dad, and Marion Chown, Tom Reichert's mother. Thus, Tom Reichert and I are first cousins. Tom is a retired dentist and very good at searching out details on his computer—on the Internet and with e-mail and letters. I'm better at actually going "on site." Together we make a great team.

Tom found that three more children were born to Robert and Mary Smith Chown in Shefford, Quebec: John James in 1834, Joseph Michael in 1840 and Mary Jane in 1842. (I think I ran into John and Joseph in Kansas and Iowa later—in my research—but we won't go into that here.) Robert and Mary had a few more kids, who appeared in the 1850 Illinois Federal Census. Robert's later naturalization request for U.S. citizenship states he entered the U.S. from Canada on June 21, 1849, at Chicago. Therefore we know our ancestors Robert and Mary emigrated from England to North America (Canada) in about 1833 or 1834 and spent the next sixteen years raising not only young William but at least three additional kids in Shefford, Quebec. (A couple of other documents list Shefford as Granby. It is located about 50 miles just south of due east of Montreal, about 50 miles north of the U.S. border.) All told, they apparently had seven children, with all except William (their first) born in Quebec. What William's life was like growing up in Quebec we do not know. Robert lists himself as "farmer" in a census of, I think, 1850. The family had always been farmers in England and would have returned to that occupation in their American future. We can only assume they were farmers in Canada. So far I have not gone to Granby to soak up the feel, sight and smell of it . . . but I intend to! At this stage we have no way of knowing what young Bill was like as oldest child in that farm family of Quebec in the 1830s and '40s. But we can begin to get a handle on him as he gets into the 1850s . . . in the U.S.A.

5

To the U.S.A.

W<small>E HAVE ON HAND (AGAIN, THANKS TO TOM REICHERT) A COPY OF ROBERT CHOWN'S</small> application for naturalization citizenship. The application itself is undated, but it was recognized by a Clerk of Court in 1885. In it the applicant, who was born in 1809, states:

> I, Robert Chown of the age of thirty-nine years upwards [he isn't sure how old he is!] do declare . . . my proper name is Robert Chown, that I was born in Devonshire County, England, . . . that I emigrated from Montreal in June 21, 1849, . . . and landed at the city of Chicago in same month, 27th day.

He goes on to renounce any past allegiances to foreign princes and potentates. . . especially to the Queen of Great Britain and Ireland . . . and "to locate myself for the present in County of Odle (Ogle) and state of Illinois." This application was actually recognized by Clerk of Court Ira Lewis, for Lee County. (This copy of Robert's naturalization request, along with a copy of the last will and testament of his grandfather Robert Chown (born in 1754), along with several other such documents are in our possession, offering absolutely fascinating ways to reach back and touch our own history.)

It is interesting to note that our William H. Chown is not listed with the family in the 1850 Illinois census. He would have been 18 years old. Why is he not there? Had he stayed back in Canada to farm on his own? Did he move to the USA with them but immediately set off on his own? In the 1860 Federal Kansas Territory Census he is shown with wife Mary E. (McGinnis) and one-year-old Mary M. Chown . . . "born in Illinois." So we know he was in Illinois in 1859 . . . or 1858. And in the 1910 Colorado census it states William and Mary had been married 53 years. So assuming they met and married in Illinois, that puts them there in 1857. Exactly where Bill was and what he was doing from about 1850-1857 (his age 25) is a guess. It seems reasonable to assume he was living on his own and probably farming. If his parents had seven children and he was the oldest, they probably felt the sooner he left the nest the better.

(I know I certainly felt that way about my kids, and we had only two! As they say, "The good life begins when the kids grow up and leave home and the dog dies." The first part is correct!)

I shall leave any more accurate research on a detailed discovery of young Bill Chown's tens, teens and early twenties to you, future reader. I know he was born in Sidbury, England, in 1832. I'm fairly certain he grew up in Granby (Shefford), Canada, from infancy to about age 18, and I'm pretty sure he spent his early 20s in Lee/Ogle counties, Illinois. Finally, I'm convinced it was there that he married Mary Ellen McGinnis around 1857 or 1858. Both Tom Reichert and I have tried to find records documenting this, but to no avail. I would love to get a grip on Mary Ellen McGinnis's family. She is listed in almost every census as having been born in Indiana in 1833, her father being from Pennsylvania, and her mother being from Kentucky. I've tried, unsuccessfully so far, to accurately pick up the McGinnis thread and see how far back and where it takes us. (After all, the McGinnis line is our last possible shot at the Mayflower!) But for this narrative, let's stick to the Chown path.

In about 1859, we have a young couple, Bill Chown and his bride, Mary Ellen, ages 25 and 24 respectively, about to start off on probably the wildest 50+-year ride any of the Chowns experienced before or since. They are in Illinois, with a just-born baby girl, Mary M. (maybe M. for McGinnis?), at a time when not just big, but huge events are unfolding in America.

Westward, Ho!

The United States of America had been founded on the premise "All men are created equal." This sentiment had sprung from negative feelings about unfairness of the class system in Europe. Feudal societies in Europe were the basis of entitlements for the "haves"—the royals and landed aristocracy—those born to their high status.

The "have nots" were automatically dealt out of any chance of success. Our founding fathers, generally considered to be one bright and ethical bunch of guys (no women of course!), put together all our great rebellion-against-the-King documents. Our Declaration of Independence and our Constitution came from English models. All the lofty brotherhood-of-man ideals contained in them actually meant everyone who was of white male European ancestry was equal. Everyone else was at least one rung down on the ladder of equality. The fact soon became obvious that we "speaketh out of both sides of our mouth" on this "all men are created equal" crap! George Washington was a slave owner. Thomas Jefferson was a slave owner. And slavery was, of course, preceded by the immediate attempt by the earliest white folks setting foot on new world soil to eradicate all savage Injuns . . . excuse me . . . Native Americans!

This country, in fact any past or future society, never has and never will be peopled by millions of "equals." The point, of course, is that all men (and women), regardless of race, religion, blah, blah, blah are supposed to have equal opportunity at success and happiness. By the 1840s and 1850s it was real clear, at least to some, that a whole bunch of our more tanned brethren really weren't getting a fair shake. The problem was exacerbated by the fact that the northern half of the old US of A was going industrial and no longer was relying on cheap manpower. The southern half not only still relied on labor, but with cotton emerging as their main product, huge numbers of slaves were required. (Cotton production is labor intensive.)

God, of course, jumped in on both sides. He whispered into abolitionist New England ears that slavery was a sinful blight. He whispered into southern ears that slavery was their rightful heritage and anyone attempting to meddle should be shot. God, obviously, is a master of supporting opposing causes. (Why else would field goal kickers and basketball foul-shooters on opposing teams all make the sign of the cross before their noble attempts at victory?) In the case of our American Civil War, I give you both John Brown, that "moulderin' in the grave" lunatic, and Stonewall Jackson, that "all is in the hands of a beneficent Providence" wacko, as personifications of my point.

Well, through the 10 to 20 years prior to the actual firing on Fort Sumter in 1861, the notion began to spring up that we could legislate control of slavery. The Missouri Compromise, The Fugitive Slave Act, and the Kansas Nebraska Act in 1851 were all attempts to control slavery and limit it where it already was . . . or was not! Missouri was already a slave state, but Kansas was still a territory in the mid- to late-1850s. The idea was that when Kansas reached statehood the voters could decide its preference on slavery. The Kansas Nebraska Act was introduced by Sen. Stephen ("Stumpy") Douglas, who figured, first, the plan was very fair and sure to solve the slave problem in Kansas and Nebraska—and would then simply be the rule to any future states—and second, it would immediately make him the head of the Democratic Party and a shoe-in for President. Only one little problem loused it up—it didn't work. Neither the rabid south nor the abolitionist north had any intention of compromising. The hatred that had built up on both sides over the previous decade had rendered backing down even an inch impossible for either side. In fact, both sides started flooding Kansas and Missouri with settlers in an attempt to affect the slave outcome. The North, fired up by abolitionist preachers and editors and financed by "emigrant aid societies" (mostly out of New England), began calling out to young men and families.

"Go West" no longer meant California; it meant Kansas, and for all those thousands of sons of Europe frozen out of hope in the Old Country or even in "back east" America. It meant cheap land; it meant excitement, hope and opportunity. One of those young couples was William and Mary Chown. They show up in the 1860 Federal Census of Territorial Kansas.

Bleeding Kansas

As mentioned, the extreme hostility and close proximity of the people on both sides of this smoldering fire pit were not going to be dampened. The Kansas "Jayhawkers," led by firebrands James H. Lane, James Montgomery and Charles Jennison, were every bit as rabble-rousing vicious as the southern "Bushwackers," led by William Quantrill, Bloody Bill Anderson and David Gregg. The North had Wild Bill Hancock; the South had Frank and Jesse James. The atrocities started in the late 1850s, running through Lane's Massacre (one man killed) at Osceola, Missouri, in 1861 and Quantrill's retaliatory massacre (every man in town killed) in Lawrence, Kansas, in 1863, finally winding up with Price's Raid and the Battle of West Port in October of 1864.

My efforts here are not meant to even modestly serve as a study of the events going on in those dark and bloody days. Cousin Tom Reichert has put together a good rendering of the military conflict as it might have been seen by our forefather, who had a brief but exciting part in it. William H. Chown's Union military record shows he was in the Kansas State Militia 6th Regiment, Company D Cavalry (probably "dismounted") under Col. James Snoddy and "Col. Jenison" (Charles Jennison). That muster was a call-up on September 20, 1864, in response to reports of an imminent raid into Kansas by the approaching Rebel Army under Gen. Sterling Price. Nothing happened.

The next call-up of William Chown's KSM 6th under Gen. Sam Curtis came October 9, 1864. This proved to be the real thing. Sterling Price had intended to make a desperation swing out of Arkansas to accomplish two goals. One, to pick up volunteers along the way for the Rebel cause in the West and, two, to keep enough pressure on Union forces in the West so the Federal Government couldn't relocate them as reinforcements in the East against Confederate Gen. Robert E. Lee. Price's invasion was originally intended to take Federal forces and supplies in St. Louis, but it failed. So General Price swung west across Missouri and took aim at West Port, Missouri (now basically Kansas City), in a last gasp effort to invade Kansas itself. Waiting for him at West Port was the Federal Army of the Border. At the very top was Gen. William Rosecrans, then Gen. Sam Curtis, Third Brigade Col. Charles Blair and KSM 6th Col. James Montgomery (succeeding Col. James Snoddy). At the very bottom were the guys holding their bayoneted British Enfields, or whatever they had, looking eyeball to eyeball at the Rebel soldiers, each trying to kill the other. One of these farmer-citizen-militia soldiers was our Bill Chown, probably mumbling to himself, "What in the Sam Hill Blazes am I doing here with dead men and dead horses all around me and minie balls whizzin' past my ears?"

In the summer of 1999, Barbara and I, with son Wally and his wife, Casey (at the time pregnant with Thomas Albert Chown III, our "Tac"), visited the field of that battle. Our William Chown and his Co. D KSM 6th were heavily involved in the Battle of West Port, sometimes referred to as the "Gettysburg of the West," on that October 23, 1864. His company was placed along the north side of Brush Creek (now in Loose Park, West Port). Directly opposite him in line of battle were the unbeaten Rebel forces under Confederate General Jo Shelby. The fighting was close in and hand to hand. And guess what . . . the good guys won!

As I said earlier, I am not really equipped to write an exhaustive military account of Price's invasion. And if I could, it would bore most of you future readers to death. Here it will suffice to say our ancestors William and Mary Chown were in that all-important wave of pioneer emigration headin' west in 1860, and they got caught up in the cataclysmic war events of bleeding Kansas.

William did, in fact, fight in combat for his country. Mary kept the home fires burning through what must have been fear beyond comprehension. We have no way of knowing Bill's exact involvement in the battle. Did he shed blood? Did he cause blood to be shed? I do know that I've almost never experienced a more spine-tingling moment than that sitting at lunch in a trendy, upscale, outdoor restaurant on the now elegantly landscaped banks of Brush Creek. Looking at my son and his wife, with a new grandbaby inside, on the very spot where my dad's grandpa gave his all so we could be having this lunch 135 years later, I felt . . . well, I can't describe it, but I'll never forget it.

Anyway, Union forces, including the militia, chased the retreating Confederate Army, now a shot-up, broken and demoralized bunch, on down the Kansas-Missouri line. There were a couple of flare ups over the next couple of days, most notably the Battle of Mine Creek on October 25, 1864. This was really the final insult to the fleeing Rebels, but I don't think William Chown was there. From what I can gather, those militia units that lived in the general Fort Scott, Kansas, area and in the path of the fleeing and rather perturbed Rebel horde, were allowed to break off the pursuit and head home fast to protect their homesteads from stray rebel pillagers. Since William and Mary Chown lived in Bourbon County and were right in the path of possible harm, I believe it likely that his active militia duty was over. Officially, his record shows he was called up for 19 days (October 7-26, 1864), was paid 53¢ per day for himself and 40¢ per day for his horse, plus a couple of dollars for clothing . . . for a grand total paid to him of $19.94. How 'bout them apples!

An interesting side note on this money: My own father, William's grandson, was Walter C. Chown I. When I was a kid, I asked him if any Chowns were in the Civil War. Due to either lack of information or lack of interest or both, my father didn't know anywhere near the story of his ancestors that we now know. But he did know "some relative was in some Civil War service, got mustered out and was home counting his military pay on the kitchen table. Somebody flung the cabin door open and the money drafted up the fireplace chimney." I'm sure this was William Chown and his $19.94!

For those of you who may have interest in a deeper understanding of Price's invasion or the conflict in Kansas-Missouri at that time, I suggest you read:

1) Cousin Tom Reichert's description
2) Gettysburg of the West, by Fred Lee
3) Action Before West Port, by Howard Monnett
4) Civil War on the Border, by Jay Monaghan
5) Quantrill and the Border Wars, by William Connelley
6) Jennison's Jayhawkers, by Stephen Starr
7) Blackflag, by Thomas Goodrich
8) General Jo Shelby, by Daniel O'Flaherty
9) Civil War in Kansas, by Albert Castrell

I hope these books and many others on the American West that in some way illuminate the life and times of our Chown ancestors will remain in my collection for your use. Now, lets move on down the trail.

Bourbon County, Kansas

Prior to our trip to Kansas/Colorado/New Mexico in 1999, I had (always with the help of cousin Tom Reichert) researched as much as possible in advance. We had copies of 1860-1885 census records showing the Chown Odyssey as it developed through Kansas and into Colorado. We also have items relating to Thomas A. Chown I's family sojourn into New Mexico, back to Colorado, and finally back east to Wisconsin. Let us pick up the thread with William and Mary after the 1864 Border War episode and continue with what we know or surmise.

The 1860 Federal Census of Territory Kansas shows them in Bourbon County, Dayton Township. To reiterate, it shows that William Henry Chown was age 27 and born in England (Devonshire, 1832). His 26-year-old wife, Mary E., was born in Indiana. In 1860 they had a one-year-old girl, Mary M. (McGinnis?), born in Illinois. (So far both Tom Reichert and I have struck out in our attempts to find any record of William and Mary Ellen's marriage, or anything on the McGinnises in Illinois from 1855-1860).

In the 1865 Kansas Census (by then a state), the William and Mary Chown family showed E.C. Chown, age four, W.R. Chown, age two, and C.G. Chown, age one—all born in Kansas. Little Mary, who would have been six years old in 1865, does not appear in the census: she was in Avondale Cemetery.

The 1870 Kansas Census shows a 16-year-old newcomer to the family: Jane F. Chown. She may have been a niece or younger sister of William. We also see a four-year-old boy, John E. Chown, plus two others: Sarah, two years old, and Frank, 2/12 (meaning, I suppose, two months). All in all, Bill and Mary apparently had seven or eight natural children, maybe a couple they "inherited," for a grand total of about ten. The 1900 Colorado census notes "ten children, seven living." We know two that didn't make it—Mary M., mentioned above, and John E., "aged 4 years 4 months 7 days," whose bodies were interred in that Avondale Cemetery. John E. must have died in 1870 or 1871, because he was listed as a four-year-old in the 1870 census, apparently dying four months and a week later.

Avondale is a long-abandoned cemetery in Devon, Kansas, just a few miles north of Fort Scott. Devon. Isn't that interesting? William was born in Devon, England. I imagine in many cases people from a given home town (in either America or Europe) migrated together. Maybe the Chowns'—not only William but also his brother John—showing up in that part of Kansas wasn't an accident. Maybe a lot of English people hailing from Devonshire founded Devon, Kansas. Who knows?

Anyway, Barb and I and Wally were trying to find that Avondale Cemetery. I had tried previously to contact the Bourbon County records office and was successful in verifying a Mary and John being buried there . . . but where the hell was it? We finally pulled the current owner of the farm that contains Avondale out of a wedding reception, and he was only too glad to spend a little time drawing a map for us.

We found it.

Avondale Cemetery is representative of what must be thousands of very old country graveyards across the Midwest dating from the mid 1800s to the early 1900s. It has only 20 or 30 grave markers in it. Some are so old and weathered you can't read them. Then you see a brand new one . . . but it's really a replacement of an old, fallen down marker. We looked and looked for a Chown, to no avail. The setting was very mournful.

It was late June, nice and warm, with a profusion of white and orange wild flowers. As I looked over this 160-acre (quarter) section, I could imagine my great grandfather as an almost-30-year-old farmer, nearly killing himself in the hot sun trying to break up the very tough native grass with a plow and mule. In my mind's eye I could see his young wife, Mary, sitting on a rude chair just outside the tiny, rough-plank or sod house they had built for their budding family. Mary would already look worn by hard labor and the brutal elements. At age 26 or 27, she probably looked like a woman 10 years older today. And I could see little Mary M. Chown at her feet, the daughter barely two years old and the mother pregnant with Elizabeth (E.C.).

As I was daydreaming, Wally yelled out, "Here it is!" I snapped back to present day. Wally had noticed a fallen and grass-encroached slab lying face up and almost unreadable. But there it was . . . Chown! Wow! Another spine-tingling moment. After we pulled back the grass and cleaned off what dirt we could, we saw "John E. Son of William H. and Mary E. Chown, died July 9, 1870, lived 4 yrs 4 months and 7 days." That was tangible proof enough we were on the right trail. It meant so much to have, not just a copy of some record in some court house, but an actual "artifact" we could touch. While we were adjusting to this major find, Wally started poking around a little white piece of concrete or stone. Just the tip was barely protruding from the ground. He dug it loose and scaled off the dirt, and we all gathered 'round to read the inscription: "MMC." There was nothing else on the stone, but we knew it was for Mary M. Chown, of course.

That about finished me off. For several years I had thought about our Chown predecessors, starting from some whimsical Norman Viking coming into England with William the Conqueror. As I have explained, in 2002 I was to go to England and touch Chown graves, seeing evidence of direct Chown ancestors back several hundred years. But that day in 1999, in that long-ago abandoned cemetery, was special. Here we had a new Chown life just waiting to be born, having all the natural, happy expectations, and at our feet I could almost feel the sorrow and grief of a young couple laying not one but two of their children in these graves. What must it have been like to be in a daily fight for survival—when every meal was hard come by, when every cough or sneeze was a possible harbinger of death and when every accident was possibly mortal? Did these children die of pneumonia or cholera, or a snakebite or a gashed leg? Who could Bill or Mary turn to for consolation other than each other? Parents? They were probably 500 miles or more away, back in Illinois or wherever. Could Bill and Mary take some "personal time" off to grieve? Hell, no. They had food to produce, clothes to mend, roof holes to patch, animals to look after, mouths to feed and myriad other duties necessary for the life of their family. Just buck up and move on! What kind of people were these two? Tougher than we can imagine.

Later in our trip we saw a statue in the old train depot yard in LaMar, Colorado, that I think well depicts mothers and wives like Mary E. Chown. It is of a fairly rugged-looking, bonneted woman standing ramrod straight, with babe in arms and a small boy clinging to her skirts. Her head is jutted forward and her eyes are focused straight ahead. She looks as though she means business and you'd best not get in her way. She is called "Madonna of the Plains." Mary Chown, I think you were such a woman, and I honor you. May blood such as your's—and of Bill's—forever course through our veins!

6

Ever Westward

To the best of my knowledge, this durable couple was in Bourbon County, Kansas (Fort Scott) from just before 1860 to just before 1880, when they moved farther west to Barber County, Kansas (Kiowa). Bourbon County, named after the Kentucky county from which its earliest pioneers hailed, is right on the Missouri border. Barber County is about 200 miles southwest and right on the Oklahoma border. The earliest homestead deed we have for William H. Chown was for the 160-acre tract back in Devon (Bourbon County), on which sits the Avondale Cemetery already described.

I return once again to the picture I conjure of a very strong and determined young couple toiling unbelievably hard to "prove up" the section over the required five years. The patent deed for "154 4/100 acres" was signed by President Ulysses S. Grant in 1872, by the U.S. Government, to William H. Chowan [sic] and recorded (way after the fact) in 1881. This deed was the first of at least a half-dozen homestead deeds from that point on into the 1920s, signed by various presidents (among them, Benjamin Harrison, Woodrow Wilson and Warren G. Harding) to William or Mary Chown or their children. But that first deed, signed by U.S. Grant, really "shivers me timbers." It brings me to a full appreciation of the part we Chowns have had in the building of America. Perhaps we don't date back to the Mayflower—but, of course, we don't really know yet how far back our McGinnis strain goes—and we don't seem to have any full-fledged heroes along the way (except of course, for you and me), but this homestead deed, signed by President Grant in 1872, at least shows we didn't just float up on some driftwood yesterday!

It is imperative that you, future Chown, physically go to some of the spots I have mentioned. Go, of course, to the four Devonshire, England, villages of Plymtree, Rockbeare, Ottery St. Mary and Sidbury. And you must go to Fort Scott, Kansas; the old fort and historic district give a fairly good feel to what Bill and Mary would have seen in the 1860s and '70s. Drive the five miles or so out to Devon where the road dead-ends at their quarter-section tract . . . and hop the fence. Avondale Cemetery is just a hundred yards or so up the dirt ruts. Pay your respects to little "MMC" and young John. Then drive up to the Linn County Courthouse. Without a doubt, Bill Chown and his Co. D 6th KSM did military drills right on that lawn, under the command of James Montgomery. And then . . . let it all soak in. Why were they there? What was their life like, with the fear and violence of the border wars . . . with the loss of two children in that far-from-home frontier? And then why, in the late 1870s, did they uproot and head farther west? Why, of all places, did they go to the end of the earth—Kiowa, Kansas?

Santa Fe Trail . . . Cowboys and Indians

I believe the answer to the above questions may include the following: 1) The lure of even more and cheaper land farther west was appealing. 2) The overall hatred, fear and violence on the Kansas/Missouri border may finally have worn them down. (The end of the Civil War— finally!—in 1865 didn't mean old Jayhawkers and Bushwackers were all of a sudden joining each other in quilting contests and barn raisings.) 3) Bill and Mary and their growing family (including their son, my grandfather, Thomas Albert Chown I, born in Bourbon County, Kansas, September 17, 1876) may merely have wanted to strike out to new territory and start afresh. (Heck, I've done that two or three times myself . . . and may do it again if I get the itch!)

Now let's figure out a couple of things. Why Kiowa, and how remote was it compared to Fort Scott? Well, the first thing to grasp is the importance of the Santa Fe Trail. This very rough route was carved out because of the need, in the 1830s and '40s, to get trade goods back and forth from Santa Fe (then Mexico) to, mainly, St. Louis. The Mexican government made it so difficult for its most-northerly citizens to buy necessities through Mexico that they turned to the USA. Very early trappers, mountain men, and frontiersmen slowly developed a strictly-commerce trail between Santa Fe and St. Louis. It became so profitable, but yet so dangerous, that two routes developed. The southern route was more direct, but had water shortages and Comanche Indians.

The more northerly route was longer and had some mountains, but less danger posed by Indians. Along that route was established Bent's Fort, a provisional stop for travelers before they headed up into the Colorado and now New Mexico mountains and then south to Santa Fe. I must declare right now that we Chowns arrived after the heyday of the Santa Fe Trail. It preceded our odyssey by 20 or 30 years. But . . . it was a very strong precursor for eventual pioneer homesteaders who would head that way. There were many wagon trains, accompanied by U.S. military escorts, that brought more and more settlers to the southwest along that historic trail, which slowly opened the whole area. Bill and Mary Chown most likely headed to Barber County, Kansas, in some kind of covered wagon . . . just like in the movies.

We have a copy of a quit claim deed dated 1876 transferring their quarter section in Bourbon County to Mr. Austin Corbin. Bill would have been about 44 years old, and Mary a year younger. She had what was to be the last of her 10 children that year—my grandfather Tom. So off they went, the two of them plus seven kids (and maybe a dog or cat), probably a few horses or mules and maybe a cow or two. And most likely they weren't alone. We have several documents serving as character references for later homestead deeds saying they had known William and his father, Robert Chown, for "28 years," which would have been back to their residing in Illinois, if not Sheffield (Grandy), Canada. I think many of these families emigrated together. I'll bet the Chown family was but one family among many in a wagon train heading farther west, all of whom knew each other. Strength and enthusiasm in numbers!

Speaking of William's father, Robert, as I said earlier, we have the list of direct male Chown lineage all the way back to Plymtree, England, in about 1540. That furthest-back Chown was named Michael, and we do actually have a copy of the handwritten Bishop's record (in old

English script), noting Michael's marriage to Miss Tamsen (Thomasine) Adams on July 21, 1569. (I mentioned this record in my account of our trip to England.) From Michael down the line to the present we've had a George, a Charles, two Williams, a couple of Walters and three Toms. (And, of course, our beloved Michael Dempsey, who brings us back full circle to Mike again. Oddly enough we had five Roberts in a row, the first born in Rockbeare, Devon, England, in 1690. He was the second Chown in a row to marry a girl named Joan. The last Robert, born in Sidbury, Devon, England, in 1809, is our Bill's dad. He would be my great-great grandfather. He was a farmer and married a young lass named Mary. (What is it with these Chown men, marrying gals with the same name as their mommas?) The fifth Robert and his Mary got hitched in 1829—I am sure in the St. Giles Church Barbara and I visited in Sidbury. And I'm sure, as well, that they lived at Furzehill Farm in Sidbury. The pictures are all in my England Photo Album for you to see. But again . . . I command you . . . go see it yourself!

It is this Robert Chown's naturalization request affidavit that I quoted at the beginning of Chapter 5. As I mentioned further, we do not know where son William was at the time. Neither do we know whether Robert's wife, Mary (William's mother), was still alive. We really don't know much about Robert. The comment years later from friends in Kiowa saying they had known Bill and his father, Robert, for 28 years is intriguing. Was Robert still back in Illinois? Did he ever move to Bourbon County, Kansas . . . or on out to Kiowa in Barber County, Kansas? We have several very old photos of Tom and Catherine Chown around 1900 and one tintype of William Chown, probably taken about the time of his Battle-of-West Port experience in 1864. Our oldest photo is of a couple, the woman on the left and the man on the right, in very old-period clothing. Both have folded hands, hers more overlapping than his. She wears a dark dress and a white, lacy head cover. He wears a dark suit and vest. Both have stern, straight-forward countenances. You know what? I think that's Robert and Mary Chown in about 1850. I recently removed it from its glued mounting and, sure enough, in my father's handwriting it says, "Parents of William Chown . . . left Illinois in 1848 . . . picture taken in 1850s . . . on way to California." Who knows if that's true, but I, at least, believe it really is Robert and Mary, my great-great grandparents.

Okay, enough of Robert. I've told you all I know about him. The beauty of all this is that it gives you future readers enough of a tantalizing track to run on; maybe you can fill in blanks and correct my many errors down the road. Let's say you are embarking on this project in 50 to 100 years . . . maybe at the turn of the 22nd century. Just think how much more information will be available and how much more computer literate you will be. (That's a term we used way back here in the early 2000s, meaning the relative ease with which one can squeeze info out of these damn computers. I personally am a zero at it; my cousin Tom Reichert is pretty good; and by 2104, you'll be terrific at it!)

Why Kiowa

Now, on to Kiowa, Kansas—more accurately, New Kiowa. I mentioned earlier that several things may serve to answer the "why Kiowa" question, one being the decades-old existence and location of the Santa Fe Trail. Another more timely phenomenon opening the doors to certain areas out West was the rapid development of a far-reaching railroad system. There wasn't just one railroad . . . many lines were competing to get their foot in the door first. The most lasting name in the Great American Southwest eventually came to be the Atchison, Topeka and the Santa Fe. We'll call it the Santa Fe. It really played a major part in our Chown saga. But as for Kiowa, the budding little town almost on the Indian Territory (now Oklahoma) line was almost killed off due to the train's . . . not going there.

When Barbara and I continued our trip in the summer of 1999, I had, again, done some pre-trip research. What we found was absolutely fascinating. This, to me, is where the William and Mary Chown family western saga really gets neat. When one thinks of the old west . . . what comes to mind? How about cowboys and Indians, wagon trains and stagecoaches, buffalo and coyotes and wolves and prairie dogs, gun fighters—according to my father, his father, Tom, actually met Wyatt Earp!—cattle drives and . . . oh! . . . how 'bout the Oklahoma Land Rush? How about Winchester '73 beaded Indian rifles . . . and navajo rugs? I know I mentioned all this earlier, but I just can't get over the fact that my own forebears were witness to all the wild and wooly western stuff I saw in the B western movies as a kid! All this and more composed the woven fiber that was a daily part of the Chown tapestry from arrival in Kiowa in about 1876 until their departure for back east in about 1917.

When Barb and I arrived in Kiowa, we had already made plans to meet with local museum curator Alice Ricke. Alice is a very amiable and helpful gal who runs the small, but fascinating, Kiowa Historical Museum. Also by sheer luck, the day we were there, Ms. Jean Brown happened in. She is the author of A History of Kiowa, Old and New, on the Cowboy Frontier, in which the William Chown family is mentioned several times. This was like not only being given a copy of "Hamlet," but also having William Shakespeare drop in to discuss it with you.

The book tells us that old Kiowa started out on the Medicine River in 1874 and struggled to make a go of it. There is some mention of Indian difficulties and attacks. Probably the first commercial purpose of Kiowa and little towns like it all over Texas, Kansas and other southwestern states involved cattle. After the Civil War, many ex-Confederates found themselves dispossessed back east and found civilized life too hard to return to. Many drifted into Texas and found huge herds of rangy, mean, but edible Spanish-descended longhorn cattle. To make a long story short, an entire industry developed in driving those cattle first all the way back to Chicago or St. Louis or even further east for slaughter, with subsequent development of railhead towns inching westward. The Chisolm Trail, by Wayne Garo, is a great and entertaining book explaining this part of the development of the West. When William Chown and family lived in Bourbon County, they undoubtedly witnessed cattle drives out of Texas.

The cattle drives created bad blood and some violence between settled farmers with local livestock and drovers of the disease-carrying longhorns moving through. Fences fell and tempers rose! As the trains kept creeping west, the wild, unruly, shoot-'em-up cowboy railhead towns kept springing up . . . and then fading. Through Kansas itself, towns like Kansas City, Abilene, Ellsworth, Wichita and, of course, the notorious Dodge City were all wild, no-holds-barred cattle-drive towns. These towns created the need for men like Batt Masterson and the Earp brothers. Kiowa sat directly below and between Wichita and Dodge City. By the time the Chowns got to Kiowa in 1876, the trail drives were certainly in evidence. The natural turbulence of trying to merge from the old, no-rules cowboy type of town to a more civilized and permanent type of community must have been a real strain.

In the early 1880s the location of the new railroad was an all important question. Would it go through the original town site, thereby assuring old Kiowa a continued shot at prospering? No, it would not. When the announcement came that the line would pass about five miles east of Kiowa, panic set in. But those earliest pioneers, Bill and Mary Chown among them, did what Americans always do . . . they improvised! They simply picked up the original wooden buildings of old Kiowa and moved them the five miles or so across the prairie to the new railroad . . . still on the Medicine River, still with a great and enthusiastic future. So in 1884 we see the birth of New Kiowa!

The aforementioned History of Kiowa, by Jean Brown, is priceless. Not only does it give a detailed description of this pioneer western town, but there are a few direct references to the Chowns. On page 24 there is a discussion of the need in January of 1885 for a bridge across the Medicine River. The existing rope-pulled ferry boat wasn't working and "four days of rotten ice" made crossing impossible. A lady and her child on a stagecoach that tipped over nearly died in a "watery grave." "William Chown's teams followed immediately and had a narrow escape from being drowned." On page 75: "William Chown's CX or 23" brand is noted in the "1897 Brand Book." On page 105 there is a mention of William Chown's being elected "president of the Kiowa Building Association" on January 1, 1884. Kiowa was becoming its own little boom town. On page 137 we read that in 1886:

> . . . the population of New Kiowa had reached 1600 and its citizens were hoping for 3000 by 1887. Main Street was the scene of continuous activity. Slow moving emigrant trains of white covered wagons passed through the city daily, moving toward the west.

And right in the forefront of the town leadership was William Chown.

Possibly not quite as stalwart a leader was Bill and Mary's number one son, Bob (lo and behold, another Robert!) On page 94, Jean Brown mentions a comical passage in The Herald newspaper around 1882 concerning normal cowboy attire with these words:

> . . . the appearance of I-Bar Johnson and Bob Chown at the Thanksgiving ball with patent leather boots, white vests and Piccadilly collars has a tendency to make the unterrified believe that the dude is rapidly wending his way to our heretofore healthful clime.

Page 30 adds to the luster of our great, great uncle Bob Chown and his friend. At a "magic lantern" exhibition, Bob and I-Bar Johnson were voted "the ugliest and laziest men in Barber County"! Hooray for us Chowns. Who says we didn't catch the eye?

Other interesting comments in the book include the fact that settlers in eastern Kansas had enough timber to build log houses. Out in Barber County they had to be content with dugouts or sod houses. Another item probably not mentioned in the real estate brochures was the presence of "large numbers of wolves, coyotes and wild hogs in the streets at night." Jean Brown quotes another local man remembering Kiowa in the 1880s as "if not quite as wild and lawless as Dodge City and Wichita . . . it was awfully close."

Another really big event occurring just outside Kiowa, Kansas, on September 16, 1893, was the famous Oklahoma Land Rush into the Cherokee Strip. We don't know whether the Chowns witnessed this historic event. Because the 1990 Federal Census was burned in a fire, we don't know where the Chown family was from 1885 to 1890. They are shown in Kiowa in

1885, and then up in Otero County, Colorado, in 1900. We do see on the back of the "torn picture" that it was taken in LaJunta, Colorado, in 1896. We don't know exactly when or why they moved. We found several deeds in Kiowa, but I believe the actual ranch, or farm, they lived on was on Sand Creek in Harper County—out toward Anthony—with maybe a townhouse in Kiowa. I found some evidence of this after we left the area. I hope to get back some day to find that ranch. But in any event, you make sure you get there someday and find it yourself. It will be good for your soul!

Page 289 of Jean Brown's book has a picture of the old Franklin School in Kiowa in 1887. I feel certain this school is where my grandfather (Bill and Mary's youngest child,) Thomas A. Chown I, attended. He would have been an infant when the family moved to Kiowa and would have had absolutely no memory of Bourbon County. Not knowing when they did, in fact, move to Otero County (La Junta), Colorado, I think it is safe to assume it was in the early to mid-1890s, since we know they were in LaJunta by 1896. There is mention of several drought years and brutally cold winters around 1895 in western Kansas. Those conditions and the desire always to keep moving west for new land may have been what prompted the move. But I think we can say that young Tom Chown had his infancy and adolescence in Kiowa, Kansas. If he was born and moved there in 1876, he would have been 19 years old if they moved to La Junta in, say, 1895.

The Baton is Passed

There will be more about William and Mary in LaJunta, but this is the point in the story where William Chown, seen as the middle car on that long train I described earlier, begins to pass the baton from those behind him to those ahead of him. Again assuming they moved in 1895, he would have been 63 years old. We know he died in 1911 at age 79, of "cancer of the face." We don't know when Mary died, but she outlived him. By the time they got to LaJunta in their mid-sixties, they must have been worn out from forty years or more of backbreaking pioneer life on the prairie. We found several homestead deeds and other real estate transactions for Mary or their children in Otero County, Colorado, but none for William. My gut feeling is that after sixty-some years of sailing to America, growing up in rural pioneer Canada, moving with his young bride to Bleeding Kansas, breaking through the untouched plains grass to grow a crop, burying two children in that sad setting, shooting at and being shot at by rebels, wagon-training further west in Kansas and helping build America while building a town through flood and drought, blizzard and scorch, locusts, tornadoes and Indians . . . William Henry Chown was "plumb wore out." God love him and Mary Ellen McGinnis Chown. What people! What incredible souls! I, of course, never knew them face-to-face, but I have come to know them, and I love them. And whether you realize it or not . . . so do you!

We have two old photos of the entire Chown family standing out on a very flat prairie. I had the better one computer-enhanced, and I was pleased to use it as the cover of this book. (It is also included in the photo section titled "Out West.") It is our oldest and very first "family photo," and to me it is priceless. I believe William and Mary are on the far left. I'm positive the heavy-set blond- or white-haired lady is Mary (based on another picture of her), and I'm 95% sure the man holding the baby (a grandchild?) is Bill. The rest of the adults would be their grown children and spouses. Also seen are young children, maybe their own and maybe grandkids.

The picture is intriguing. Note the similar clothing of the women. Note the free spirit up on the windmill. Bill is casual in his shirt sleeves. A couple of the men are less casual in dark suits. The guy fourth from left with suspenders and floppy hat may be son Bob. This is pure speculation, but Bob was, to the best of our info, somewhat of a goof . . . and this guy looks to me as though he fits the bill. Depending on when this picture was taken, one of the young boys is likely to be my grandfather Tom. Due to the dead-flat horizon, this location has to be Kiowa or LaJunta. If the location is Kiowa in, say, 1885 or so, the boy sitting in the foreground, or one of the boys on horseback, could be a nine-year-old Tom. If the photo was taken closer to 1895, in either place, the guy dead center dressed in a black suit with his right arm cocked back could be a 19-year-old Tom. That could be his 30-year-old brother, Charlie, three people to his right. And who are the two people barely visible in the buggy to the far right? Fascinating . . . absolutely fascinating, dear reader. Look real hard at this picture. It is the first actual look we get of Michael Chown and Tamsen Adams, of all those Roberts . . . and Janes, Joans and Marys . . . and of what will be Walters and Lisas and Toms and Michaels and Megans and Kates and Mary Macs . . . all future Chowns and Reicherts and many more. Yep, take a real good look. These people are you and me. This picture is us!

Before we reluctantly leave Bill and Mary behind, let me impart another interesting anecdote about them. William Chown filled out and signed an affidavit on September 8, 1883, called a "pre-emption proof-testimony of claimant" form. It was done in Anthony (Harper County), Kansas. I am pretty sure, as mentioned earlier, their homestead wasn't actually in Kiowa (Barber County) but immediately to the east in Anthony (Harper County). Kiowa, however, was still the larger commercial center of the area. Anyway, this form was Bill's attempt to lay claim to the quarter section (160 acres) he was farming. Here are some of the questions and answers excerpted from the completed form:

> Name and age?
> > William H. Chown, 51 years
> Are you head of family?
> > Yes, wife and 6 children
> When did you first settle land?
> > June 18, 1882 [This wasn't his first home in the Kiowa area.]
> What was first act of settlement?
> > building a house
> Any improvements on existing land you settled?
> > none
> What improvements have you made, and value of same.
> > have a log house 16' x 18', kitchen 12 'x 12', well, 2 corrals,
> > and a branding pen . . . value $400[1]
> Use of land?
> > grazing and cutting hay and home
> How much land broken and cultivated . . . what crops raised?
> > none . . . it is too sandy for farming and would be of little use
> > to plant

This tells us two things. Bill may have been a crop farmer back in Bourbon County—east Kansas—but the name of the game in west Kansas was ranching—animal grazing . . . live

---

[1]This seems to contradict the documented fact that trees were scarce in Kiowa. It's too late to ask Bill.

stock. It also sheds light on the opulent lifestyle they were enjoying in 1883 frontier Kansas, six children and two adults in a 16' x 18' log house? Wow! Where on earth did they put the king-size bed?

Today we can scarcely imagine life without the microwave, the sub-zero refrigerator, the Jacuzzi, the pool table and the entertainment center. And could we cope without the two- or three-car garage? We just can't get a grip on the Spartan existence they had there and then. But we must force ourselves to realize and never forget that our much more comfortable lifestyle of the 21st century is standing squarely on their shoulders.

7

On to LaJunta

ONE OF ONLY A COUPLE OF MEMORIES MY FATHER, WALTER, RELATED ABOUT HIS GRANDFATHER, William, was in LaJunta. My father was born in 1903, and his grandfather died in 1911. Their lives overlapped by only eight years. Since the Tom and Catherine Chown family didn't live in LaJunta, Wally probably laid eyes on his grandparents only a few times . . . maybe Christmas visits. But one visit obviously made quite an impression on young Wally. Let's see how close I can come to retelling it the way Wally used to. Imagine him telling it the way he had seen it, from the perspective of a small boy. These are his words as closely as I can recall them (with a few interruptions by me).

We were all gathered at my grandparents' ranch one time. It was extremely cold. [Christmas?] My grandfather [William] had recently imported a pair of greyhounds from England for hunting coyotes. After a full day we all went to bed. Sometime after midnight the dogs started kicking up a ruckus and woke the whole household. When we all gathered in the barnyard in our nightshirts, the scene we beheld was as follows. There, silhouetted in the full moon on the very apex of the barn roof, was a very large bobcat. When either my dad or one of his brothers suggested they shoot it off the roof, my grandpa stopped them short. He said this was a golden opportunity to demonstrate the skills of these two very expensive greyhounds.

His plan was simple. He, himself [probably then about 75 years old] would shinny up the barn roof to the top . . . and then creep along the roof-line toward the bobcat. Tom, my father, and his brothers— Frank, Charlie and Bob—would be controlling the dogs down on the ground. Grandpa, having gotten close to the cat, would then make a lunge at the creature, who would, of course, back off the roof into oblivion and be torn to pieces by the waiting canines. And lunge Grandpa did. But as in all the "best laid plans of mice and men," one expected result didn't pan out. The bobcat did not back off the roof. In fact, he jumped right over Grandpa's head onto his back, clawing and "ppffttting" furiously. In his attempt to gain traction on Grandpa, the cat proceeded to totally shred Grandpa's nightshirt and remove it

51

completely from his back before racing down and off the other end of the barn to freedom!

Of course our eyes were momentarily diverted, following the cat's escape route. But when we refocused on the remaining scene on the roof . . . well, all I can say is it was a sight to behold. A vision I will never forget of my dear grandpa Bill. There he was, naked as at the moment of birth, back all scratched and bleeding, straddling the roof-line and all in full moonlight silhouette. Well, we on the ground were all dumbstruck by the scene. I was so young, only five or six, that I was non-comprehending. But my father and uncles began to react, first with chuckles, then guffaws and finally out and out roaring hilarity. But what followed punctuated the scene and emblazoned it into my memory forever. Grandpa must have had a terrible temper, because after climbing, naked and bleeding, down off the barn, he, without a word, grabbed a double-barreled shotgun from one of his sons and shot both dogs dead.

End of story. Now let's think about this a minute. Could this story possibly be true? I had never heard of greyhounds being hunters, which made me skeptical, but I was amazed to read on page 144 of Jean Brown's History of Kiowa that in 1887 a certain Col. D.R. Streeter had "six greyhounds trained to catch a wolf by the throat, hounds so fast no wolf could escape." So the premise of hunting greyhounds seems to be correct. As to the rest of the story . . . could you make that up? It is also interesting to realize that William and Mary—if they did have a ranch house large enough to sleep several families at Christmas, as well as a barn and money enough to buy two greyhounds—had certainly progressed well past their 16' x 18' log house of 1883!

One of the only other memories my father had of William and Mary involved their disapproval of their son Tom's marrying Catherine Rodden, my grandmother. The reason for their disdain and dislike for her? She was Irish Catholic! Their religious tradition would have been Protestant Church of England—Anglican. Whether they were church-goers or not we don't know. But they sure had a dim view of Catholics and Irish. This manifested itself in two ways to young Wally Chown, their grandson. He remembered his grandmother Mary—whom he loved and remembered as an old, white-haired, kindly lady—gave him a burro. We still have a picture of him with it. He was seven. Within a week or so one of his aunts came and retrieved it because she didn't like her sister-in-law, Wally's mother, the Catholic. Go figure.

I remembered the conflict recently on a trip Barbara and I made to Ireland. It caused me to write the following short poem. Please indulge me.

> Thomas Chown's is a schizophrenic life,
> Half English, half Irish creates terrible strife.
> Whichever side I boast . . . or roast . . .
> I love or hate myself the most!

The other evidence my father offered for this family conflict was the torn family photo we have. It was apparently the William and Mary Chown family in 1896 . . . in LaJunta. It has been torn so that only mother Mary (seated) and 20-year-old son Tom and a sister are shown.

My father's understanding was that Tom had later been "torn out of the family" for marrying a Catholic. As with all family differences . . . who knows? It may have been true or it may have been a distortion of fact to a little boy. But I do know one thing—I'd give almost anything to have the rest of that picture!

The last thing I can think to relate about William and Mary is with regard to their grave site in LaJunta, which Barbara and I visited in 1999. We went to the oldest section of Evergreen Cemetery and found their graves. The stone says "Chown . . . Father, Mother, age 80 years . . . gone but not forgotten." No actual names or dates, which seems odd. We have William's death certificate, but not Mary's.

The information on Bill's death certificate was attested to by his son Frank, but why so vague and undated? We'll never know. Another interesting fact about the grave is the name "Dwyer" on the backside. We know a strong Chown-Dwyer family relationship and friendship went way back to Kiowa . . . maybe even to Bourbon County. Two of Bill and Mary's daughters married Dwyers. And they're all buried together in Evergreen Cemetery . . . interesting.

The only photos we have of William are the old one at the front of this narration taken with his banner around his chest, probably in 1864, and the almost unrecognizable one in the family photo on the prairie where he's holding the baby. As for Mary, we have the same prairie picture. Then we also have the "torn off picture," with a daughter and son Tom. It's really quite clear and a good picture of her. I think I see my father in her face, but maybe it's just because I want to. The last photo of Mary is quite poignant. She is on a porch in a rocking chair, dressed in a black dress with a white lace collar. She looks serene. Someone wrote "Grandma Chown . . . 81" on the bottom. She would have been 81 in 1915, four years after William's death in 1911. They would have been married about 53 years when Bill died. On the back of this photo she herself wrote "Mother at 81 to her baby boy." That's why we have this picture. Her "baby boy" was my grandfather Tom. We don't know exactly when Mary died. We hope to eventually find her death certificate.

I realize I keep dragging out the William and Mary part of this saga, but now I swear I'm done with them. It's just that I'm so bowled over by their lives. My own sense of religion has nothing to do with the normal Judeo/Christian baloney of heaven and hell and crosses and popes and saints and turning the other cheek and above all else dropping a lot in the collection plate before you go home and gossip about your neighbors. But I do consider myself, somehow, "spiritual." I think we came here from somewhere . . . and we're going somewhere after this life. My hope is we get to join a "stream of consciousness" type of time flow. I'd like to be able to press forward or reverse and actually be at any human event in our collective past or future. I'd love to know, for example, what happens to our American citizenry over the next couple of hundred years. I wonder if we'll ever recapture any sense of self-responsibility. (I also wonder if OSU basketball will ever recapture the greatness of the Lucas/Havlicek years . . . but I digress.)

I would be even more desirous of going back in time. I'd love to know if Pheidippides really made that long run. Did Shakespeare really do the writing or did Marlowe? Why in the hell did Lee order that absolutely stupid charge on the third day at Gettysburg? And whether I could do it in the past, present or future. I'd love the opportunity somewhere along the line to kick the ass of Bill Clinton, the worst president in the history of the United States. (But again, I digress.)

What I really hope in my crazy vision of the afterlife is that I could, just for a moment, visit with my past people. I'd like to have a beer with Bill Chown. I'd like to ask him about West Port and sod busting and just pioneering in general. And if I could, just for a moment, I'd visit with Mary. I'd do what I think my father would do. I wouldn't ask her much. I'd just like to kiss her forehead, give her a big hug and thank her so very, very much!

PLATE 13. GREAT-GREAT GRANDPARENTS OF THE AUTHOR. Robert and Mary Chown, the parents of William H. Chown. Robert was born in Sidbury, England, in 1809. He and Mary brought young son, William, to Canada around 1834; they entered the United States at Chicago on June 27, 1849. This photograph, probably taken in the early 1850s, is the oldest Chown photo in the author's possession.

PLATE **14**. GREAT GRANDPARENTS OF THE AUTHOR. William Henry and Mary Ellen (McGinnis) Chown. The photo of William was probably taken in Kansas at the time of the Battle of West Port in October 1864. We are not sure what the chest banner signifies, but it probably has something to do with his "Jayhawker" leaning. The original photo is a tintype. The photo of Mary, extracted from "the torn picture," was taken in LaJunta, Colorado, in 1896—more than 30 years after the tintype of William was taken.

Plate 15. THE TORN PICTURE—taken in 1896 in LaJunta, Colorado. This is our first photo of Thomas A. Chown I, shown here at age 20. His mother, Mary Ellen, is seated to his right; she was 62. Standing at Tom's right is one of his sisters, either Elizabeth or Olive. The man at her right is either their brother or her husband.

PLATE 16-A. FAMILY FARM IN KIOWA, KANSAS, AND SANTA FE RAILROAD STATION IN COLORADO.

Top: To the best of our knowledge, this Chown photo was taken some time during the 1890s on their farm (also cover photo).

Bottom: The Santa Fe Railroad Station and Harvey House in LaJunta, where Catherine first met Tom. This is the site of the horrible lynching episode in 1902.

PLATE 16-B. REVISITING THE OLD WEST IN 1999—*above*, Tom II and Wally II finding graves of Chown children in Avondale Cemetery in Bourbon County, Kansas: *below*, Tom II with Jean Brown, author of *A History of Old Kiowa*, and, on his left, Alice Ricke, who runs the Kiowa Historical Museum.

PLATE 17.
CATHERINE
RODDEN CHOWN.
This photograph
may have been taken
around 1900 back in
Wisconsin, prior to
Catherine's going
west, but it is
possible that it was
concurrent with her
marriage to Tom
Chown I in 1903.
Either way, she was
a truly beautiful
young woman.

PLATE 18. GRANDPARENTS OF THE AUTHOR. Tom and Catherine Chown. This is most likely their wedding photo, taken in 1903, in LaJunta, Colorado.

PLATE 19. TOM AND SON.
Thomas A. Chown I with infant son, Walter C. Chown I, about a year old . . . 1904.

PLATE 20. MASTER WALTER CORVILLE CHOWN I.

Top: As anyone can see from this photo, Walter was a "going places" guy; here he is about four years old, around 1907.

Bottom: Walter, at seven, and the burro he had for a brief time in 1910 at Pictou, near Walsenburg, Colorado.

PLATE 21.
WALLY AND MARION.

Top: Eight-year-old Wally and five-year-old Marion at a school picnic in Pictou, Colorado, 1911. Wally is standing near the top on the far left. Marion is second from left on the front row (behind the dog).

Bottom: Marion at four and Wally at seven in a serial photo common at the time.

PLATE 22. CATHERINE, TOM AND MARY.

Top, right: Tom and Catherine, probably some time around 1910 or 1915 in Pictou, although the photo could have been taken in an earlier mining camp like Las Vegas or Madrid, New Mexico.

Above: Catherine (standing second from right) as a Red Cross volunteer in Walsenburg, Colorado. This photo was probably taken in front of Huerfano County Courthouse, c. 1915.

Right: Our last photo of Mary Ellen McGinnis Chown, at age 81, taken in LaJunta in 1915. The caption on the back reads, "Mother at 81 to her baby boy." That baby boy was Thomas A. Chown I, the author's grandfather.

8

Tom and Catherine

I HAVE CHOSEN TO TELL THIS STORY OF CHOWN WANDERINGS DOWN THROUGH THE AGES FROM the vantage point of couples . . . not merely the men. In western civilization family continuity is delineated by the male's surname, a system patently unfair to women, but a system born of necessity for some kind of chronological order. We indeed go from grandfather to father to son to grandson, with no automatic inclusion of our women. I can't help noticing, though, that Tamsen Adams' name is written in those Bishops Records from the 1500s right beside Michael Chown's. I guess it is true that only the male's bloodline comes directly down the surname, with each wife/mother bringing in a fresh new mix of genes. Someone told me if we go back twenty generations, each of us has a million ancestors. Could be; I'm too lazy to do the math. The point is, through female inclusion, or adoption, or even what happened in the hay mow that was never fessed up to, we all go back to Adam and Eve (or those first two apes, depending on your preference).

But getting back to our ladyfolk, as mentioned, I strongly believe that Mary Ellen McGinnis "Madonna-of-the-Plains" Chown was every bit the force that husband William was. And as we will see, most of these past Chown men had a habit of marrying strong women who, in their own right, had very interesting stories. Consider the personalities and background of Thomas Albert Chown I and Catherine Rodden and the way their paths crossed.

We have already stated that Tom Chown was born in 1876 in Dayton (Bourbon County), Kansas, near Fort Scott, and immediately moved to Kiowa. He grew up in that truly wild west cow town and must assuredly would have developed a rough and tumble personality with strong anti-Mexican, anti-Catholic, anti-Indian tendencies—most likely a hit-first-and-ask-questions-later type of guy. The torn-picture photo shows him to have been a strikingly handsome young buck when the family moved to LaJunta in his late teens. He was six feet, two inches tall and, in his youth, weighed about 190 pounds. He appears to have had dark, wavy hair, and he had blue eyes. According to his son, my father, he was a leader . . . a personality . . . an outrageous "presence."

Catherine Rodden couldn't have come from a more opposite background, on the surface. She was born in Cascade (or Mitchell), Wisconsin, near Sheboygan, in 1878 to Michael and Mary Rodden—Irish Catholics. In 1850 Michael, at about age 18, had immigrated from

Ireland. Five years later he married Mary Murphy, on February 2, 1855, at Holy Name Church in Sheboygan. Their children numbered 16, with Catherine Rodden being the 13th child, born March 30, 1878. Years later, in a poem she wrote out west, she clearly showed how much she had enjoyed her childhood.

Memories
Back again to old Wisconsin
That is where I long to roam,
Back among the hills of Mitchell
To the place where I was born.

Playing farm upon the hill-side
Where the sun shines bright and warm
With my sisters and my brothers
With no thought of care or harm.

Making bonnets out of leaves
Leaves from the hickory tree
Picking wild flowers on the hill-side
And chasing the bumble bee.

I think I hear my mother singing
In the cottage down below
Singing softly to the baby
As she rocks her to and fro.

Oh, I long for just one moment
When the moon is shining still
To sit and to think and to listen
To the song of the Whip-poor Will.

But tonight I am sad and lonely
In my far off western home
And my thoughts keep drifting backwards
To that dear old child-hood home.
Mrs. Thos. Chown

The Harvey Girl

But there was something different about Catherine, especially for the times. She left the relative comfort and security of her family farm life to become a . . . Harvey Girl! If you have never heard of the Harvey Girls, you should read The Harvey Girls: Women Who Opened the West, by Lesley Poling-Kempes. Since you probably cannot put your hands on a copy of the book right this minute, let me give you a quick rundown.

As the trains began poking farther and farther west, day excursions for tourists got more difficult. Although the trips got longer and longer, there were no eating or sleeping accommodations on the trains. In 1876 the Santa Fe Railroad folks began paying attention to a guy named Fred Harvey, who had opened a tiny lunch counter in the Topeka, Kansas, depot. By 1880 they had struck a deal with him to open restaurants along the Santa Fe's expanding routes, all the way from Chicago to Galveston, Texas. The waitresses in these restaurants were called Harvey Girls. Poling-Kempes explains in her book how refined these girls were required to be, dressed in "immaculate black and white uniforms." Eventually, Harvey Houses were built at the main stopping-off tourist sites, and some were quite elaborate hotels. The ones at Grand Canyon, Santa Fe and San Diego were among them.

The interesting thing about the early Harvey Girls (they existed from the 1880s through the 1950s) is twofold. First, being a Harvey Girl was one of the only "respectable" ways for a young single woman to leave home. Ladies did not "go off to college," or "take a job," or "just kick around the country" in the late 19th century or early 20th century. And it is pretty well documented that the only single women out west back then were either Indian squaws or prostitutes. The incursion of all these young eastern girls into Kansas, Colorado, New Mexico, Texas and beyond had a major impact on bringing at least a modicum of softness and civility to these wild cowboys, miners and hooligans. And it gave literally thousands of bored-stiff but adventuresome young gals an otherwise impossible chance to "see the world."

The second result of the Harvey phenomenon was what happened when they got out west. Many stayed! It is said in the book that the Harvey girls actually "populated the west." An awful lot of current-day folks out there had Harvey Girl great grandmothers. Well, dear reader, you're one of 'em!

I've been unable to find any written record on Catherine Rodden's Harvey employment but have a pretty good idea what happened via my father Walter's explanation. It goes something like this:

Catherine was probably a typical, restless young lady on the farm in the late 1890s. Along about 1900 she either saw an ad or someone told her about the "Harvey Girl" possibility. We don't know whether she went with her parents' reluctant semi-approval or with their enthusiastic blessing (one less mouth to feed), but it is most likely that she signed on in Chicago. The pictures we have of her at about that time show a comely young lady . . . quite statuesque. In one photo she is standing alone in a long, dark dress. We always assume their clothing was black because the photos were all black and white, but her dress may have been dark blue or green or maroon. Her hands are behind her back. In another photo she and Tom are together . . . a very handsome couple . . . probably a wedding picture. They were probably married in late 1902 or early 1903, but that's getting ahead of the story.

Catherine did, in fact, become a Harvey Girl right at the turn of the century. She was about 22. We don't know how long she was thus employed before arriving in one of the Santa Fe Harvey House towns—LaJunta, Colorado.

A Man of the West

Tom Chown was a strapping young man of the West who was about age 24 or 25. According to the 1900 census in LaJunta, Colorado, he was living, then, with his parents.

During the year after my father's death in December, 1969, I composed a narrative about him and our family as he had revealed the Chowns to me. This manuscript informs much of what I have written here concerning my paternal grandparents, Tom and Catherine, and my father, Wally. One of the first things I recall his telling me about his parents was the strange situation my grandmother walked into when she arrived in LaJunta and the bizarre way she and Tom Chown met.

There were Harvey Houses in the train depots, and she arrived in La Junta, Colorado, on theSanta Fe to work in the Harvey House. As she stepped off the train a group of young, boisterous men were lynching a Negro man for some trumped up charge having to do with molesting a white woman. The leader of the hangmen was Thomas Chown. Catherine despised this type of behavior and would have nothing to do with Tom. A night or two later they met at a dance, and he sweet-talked her into meeting him outside in his buggy. As she went out the front door, he ran out the side door smack into an apple tree and knocked himself unconscious.

There are probably errors or misunderstandings in the evolution of this story over the past century, but the basic punch line is that my grandfather, Thomas A. Chown I, was ringleader of a lynch mob that hanged a black guy in the Santa Fe depot in about 1900 or so. Putting the dance and the apple tree aside . . . can you think of a more god-awful event to have in one's heritage? I was able to set it aside as a probable exaggeration until Barb and I visited LaJunta in 1999. We visited the terrific Otero County Museum and, in passing, bought A History of Otero and Crowley Counties, by Frances Bollacker Keck. I read it cover to cover, and I recommend it to you.

To my astonishment, I read about a historical event that thoroughly shook me. In a chapter on the historical ethnic mix in Otero, page 349 is specifically about black Americans. The discussion relates to the generally good life blacks had in LaJunta, although "they were never a large percentage of the population." The quote continues:

> There was only one example of racial conflict. In 1902 a black American railroad worker named Wallace was accused of raping a white woman. He was convicted of the crime, and in a riot, soon afterward, a gang of citizens managed to remove the man from the jail and hang him [my emphasis] from a light pole on the corner of Third Street (Then Kansas Avenue) and Santa Fe Avenue.

Wow . . . double wow! If this "one example," which almost exactly matches up with the story my dad passed down isn't the same event, it's sure the coincidence of the century. I don't think we can accurately pass judgement on this atrocity of long ago, for it was a different age and different time. But we may not want to be too high and righteous as to where our heritage has been.

Starting a Family

With that outlandish beginning behind them, Tom and Catherine got married, apparently in late 1902. I don't think they ever lived as a couple in LaJunta. He was 26 in 1902 and worked as an engineer for the Santa Fe. A discrepancy of my father's birth date arose, but we do know he, their first child, was born in Amarillo, Texas in 1903. He always thought his birth date was December 22, but his birth certificate, which he and I found in Santa Fe at Our Lady of Guadalupe Church in 1965, said June 22, 1903. I can only suppose they were living in Amarillo, but it is possible they just happened to be in Amarillo—another Santa Fe Harvey House town—when Catherine gave birth to Walter.

Maybe the family strife over her being Catholic forced her and Tom to move away from LaJunta, but their entire life together out west was in railroad or mining towns in New Mexico and Colorado, not LaJunta. The only photo we have relating to Amarillo is a tiny, wrinkled picture of a small adobe house. On the back it says "house Walter Chown born in." Who knows? We do know young Walter's earliest memories were of Madrid, New Mexico. In 1904, Madrid was listed as place of residence on his birth record at Our Lady of Guadalupe.

There is a bit of confusion as to Tom's occupation. In a clipping from a Las Vegas, New Mexico, paper in about 1900, he is described as "a Santa Fe engineer." This news article identifies Tom only as a hero who literally "saved the train."

> Bravery on the part of Thomas Chown, a Santa Fe engineer residing at 317 Grand Avenue probably averted a serious accident on the Santa Fe near Watrous last night. As a result of his self sacrifice and devotion to duty Chown, badly burned from escaping steam, is confined to his bed at his home. He is being attended by Dr. E.B. Shaw, Santa Fe physician.
>
> Chown with fireman Gregory, left here last night on a Santa Fe freight of which conductor Reardon was in charge. At Watrous the engine was uncoupled and run up to Shoemaker to take water. The train being left on the siding [sic]. On the return a pipe broke filling the cab with escaping steam. The brakeman jumped and escaped injury.
>
> Chown stayed at his post. He climbed outside the cab and reached through the window with his left arm and seized the throttle. He was unable to entirely stop the engine. Turning about he thrust his right arm into the mass of escaping steam and succeeded in forcing the throttle shut, stopping the engine. The engine was backing when the accident occurred and had Chown jumped it probably would have collided with the Chicago Limited, east bound No. 4, which was due in a short time. The accident occurred at 11:45 p.m.
>
> Chown's injuries consist of extensive burns on his arms, legs and head. They are not serious, but probably will keep him at home for several days.

By looking closely at the original clipping, one can see the hint of a time frame. Barely discernible at the bottom are the words "to greet Roosevelt." I am sure the reference is to Teddy Roosevelt's coming back to a Las Vegas "Rough Rider" reunion some time in the period 1900-1903. Tom's railroad watch mandatory time service verification in 1911 lists him as an engineer. Yet my father always said they lived in coal mining towns and Tom worked as a "combustion engineer," putting in mining equipment. I am guessing the answer is that he was both. I think he was employed by the Santa Fe the whole time as a train engineer, but also hired out as an independent contractor to the coal mines. My father said he was almost sure his dad had an engineering degree from a Kansas Mineral and Mining school, a forerunner, he thought, to the University of Kansas or Kansas State University.

To describe Catherine and Tom's life out west during the years 1903-1917, I rely on what my father told me about his life as a young boy . . . that is, what I was able to recollect when I wrote my 1970 narrative.

After Tom and Catherine were married and Walter (my father) was born, he was christened Walter Corville Chown. As you might suppose, this name forced Wally to be able to defend himself at a very early age. Actually, according to his birth record at Our Lady of Guadalupe Church in Santa Fe, he was christened with the hispanic version of his name: Gualterio Chown 6/19/04 . . . and DOB 6/22/03. The name Walter Corville Chown has an amusing history itself. When Walter was born, the man to whom Catherine had been engaged in Cascade or Milwaukee sent out a case of champagne to the proud parents. Tom thought anybody who was big enough in spirit to send champagne to his former fiancée and the man who had stolen and married her, must be one hell of a man. The man's last name was Corville. Hence, Tom named his son Walter Corville Chown after an ex-suitor of his wife.

9

Memories of a Lad Out West

WALLY GREW UP IN COAL MINING TOWNS, PRIMARILY BECAUSE HIS FATHER TOM AT FIRST worked as an engineer and a fireman on the Santa Fe Railroad but later became an engineer putting in the mining equipment and tipples in coal mines. By his own account, Wally went to sixteen different grade schools. This background forced him to become something of a fist-fighter. Years later he became the heavyweight champion of Marquette Academy (high school). In fact, all through his life and into his 50s and 60s he was known to have scrapes with people who angered him a little too much. In his grade school days, every school he attended had a hierarchy of the toughest guys. He would have to fight one of them and work his way up or down the ladder until he found his niche. In one of the towns he became an arch-enemy of a Mexican named Juan Garcia. (I have since learned that almost every Mexican is named Juan Garcia.) Juan was responsible for deliberately setting up logs on a railroad track where Wally and his sister, Marion, were hand-pumping one of the little portable cars. When the car hit the logs, the car went off the tracks, and Wally and Marion were injured somewhat. That was reason enough to create enmity, but Juan Garcia also shot my father in the knee with a .22 rifle. He kept the scar for life.

I don't know the sequence of a lot of the stories my father remembered. Some of them just flash back into my memory as very typical events that might occur in the life of a small boy in the early 20th century American West. Once when Wally was probably younger than 10, some older boys told him that the railing on a bridge going over a creek tasted very good, like peppermint. Unfortunately it was in the middle of the winter with temperatures below freezing. When Wally placed his tongue on the bridge to find out, it immediately froze to the bridge. He was in that perplexing condition for some time until his father came with a torch and heated the bridge to the point where it finally melted and released the boy. No more tasting bridges for him for the rest of his life.

Wally remembered his dad pitching baseball on different mining town teams. One of the earliest towns in which Wally lived was MADrid, New Mexico, just southeast of Santa Fe. Actually, it should be pronounced MaDRID, but according to my father the white Anglo-Saxon Americans went out of their way to mispronounce all the Spanish words. The Mexicans were considered the minority group, and everybody bent over backward to insult or embarrass them whenever possible. There is a Raton Pass on Route 25 in New Mexico in the mountains, just below Trinidad, Colorado. Dad claimed that everybody pronounced it RATune pass, again to insult the Mexicans.

When I visited Madrid with my father in 1965, I noticed that even though it was deserted and an old ghost town, some of the original buildings were still there from the early 1900s. There were posters and bulletins in these buildings instructing the miners of different events. The oddity was that these bulletins were printed in five or six different languages. My father explained that this was a very common thing in some of the extremely remote mining towns. Hard core criminals—that is, murderers, rapists, robbers and thugs of every type—had come from many different countries to escape the law. A town such as Madrid, New Mexico, was about as remote as any place on the face of the earth. They believed they would never be found in these towns. Consequently the railroad or the mining management had to print up bulletins in the languages these men could read. My father did not have very many memories of the town of Madrid because he was very young when he lived there. (Barbara and I visited Madrid in 1999. What a difference! It is now an "artsy fartsy" ghost town!)

The next town he remembered was Pictou, Colorado. It is near Walsenburg, which is probably about a hundred miles south of Denver. Although there were many different towns in which my father lived for periods of anywhere from six months to a couple of years, time had blurred his memory of his early youth. Pictou, which is now just a shambles of the buildings that were once there, was a real going town in the early 1900s. My father had many memories of this town. He remembered such things as his first drink of whiskey (which, incidentally, was to be followed through his lifetime by many more). He remembered that he and a friend, probably both about seven or eight years old, were walking down a dirt road one day. A man went by with a horse and wagon. The two boys jumped on the back of the wagon, unnoticed by the man. Finding part of a pint of whiskey, the boys sat in the back of the wagon trying to taste it, only to be interrupted by the man when he turned around and saw what was happening. With abusive language, the man chased the boys out of the wagon and up the hill.

Speaking of whiskey reminds me of Wally's recollection of a Pictou dirt road known as Hell's Half Acre. When we were there in 1965, we could still see the remains of the seven saloons in a row that my father used to talk about. Miners are not a quiet or introspective lot. They can raise hell when they want to. I suppose they felt that if this street needed any buildings, seven saloons would be satisfactory. The Chown mansion (a company shack) was on a hill probably 300 feet from this street. One day a man came to visit Tom, and Wally saw them sitting on the porch, talking. Somebody yelled up from the town that several of the miners had this man's son pinned to one of the walls of a saloon, shooting at him. The man grabbed the rifle out of his horse holster, jumped on the horse and went riding down the hill, shooting at these men. Most of them got mounted and got away, but one of them was pinned behind a wall before he could get to his horse. Every time he would run out, Tom's friend would shoot at him. Finally the culprit made it to his horse and rode away without being shot.

On another occasion, Wally noticed another man visiting his father; they were talking in the toolshed beside their house. A Mexican walked into the toolshed with his sombrero held in front of him. All of a sudden he pulled a knife from behind the sombrero and lunged at the man visiting Tom. The Mexican and the visitor started racing around the yard, the Mexican, with knife in hand, chasing Tom's friend. Just as the Mexican was closing in, he stepped into a wagon rut and fell. The fall carried his knife hand to the victim, but the knife buried itself only an inch into the man's back. If the rut hadn't been there, Tom's friend would probably have been killed.

Tom came up behind the Mexican and broke a 2x4 over his head. The blow did not knock out the Mexican, but it did daze him, and he wandered off in a sort of haze. These types of stories appear violent and foreign to us now, but they were fairly commonplace in those days. If you didn't like somebody, it was just as easy to smack him in the teeth as tell him you didn't like him, I suppose.

Another interesting father/son experience occurred during a blizzard that was written up in one of the local newspapers. Wally thought this actually happened in LaJunta. Tom and young Wally, probably on a visit to Tom's parents' ranch, were out in their horse-drawn wagon when the blizzard hit. They got lost and could not make it home. The snow piled up, and finally Tom realized they could go no further . . . shortly after noticing that a pack of wolves had begun to follow them. As the situation got more desperate and more wolves started following, Tom put Wally up in a tree. He then took out a .22 rifle—which I still have and my son, Wally, will probably have—and shot the lead wolf. The others evidently took that as a good enough bluff and turned around and left. Tom then lifted his son out of the tree, and they found their way to a neighbor's ranch where they spent two or three days before they could get home.

Catherine—and several others, apparently—thought her husband and son had perished in the blizzard. There was an article in the paper stating they had died in the storm. (Dad and I spent some time in a LaJunta newspaper office in 1965 looking for that article . . . to no avail. He was too vague on the actual date.)

Wally used to have an affinity for dogs. He got a lot of humorous moments out of relating adventures his dogs had gone through. He remembered a dog named Shep crawling under the house they lived in and getting bitten by snakes, puffing up and going off some place in the prairie and just lying there, miserable, for two or three days. He got better and came back, but the cycle was repeated several times over a year or two, until finally he became immune to the snake bites and they didn't seem to bother him.

Another "Shep" story Wally used to tell was about a cowboy and his trusted dog, Shep. They were lost in the mountains, and there was nothing to eat. "It got so bad after starvin' for four days," lamented the cowboy, "I finally had to kill ol' Shep and eat him. And the worst part," he continued, "was as I sat there finishin' him off by the campfire, I just couldn't stop thinkin' how much ol' Shep would've enjoyed those bones!" Hearty har, har!

Wally remembered seeing a bullsnake fighting with a rattlesnake. The fight went on and on, and finally the bullsnake got the rattler by the tail and just slowly swallowed him, the rattlesnake writhing and fighting until his head finally disappeared down the head of the bullsnake. I am inclined to take that one with more than a grain of salt, although you never knew exactly what you could believe from Wally. He had a way of mixing 10% truth with 90% horse manure, arriving at a palatable blend.

One story harked back to a day when Wally, as a boy, was berry-picking near a dry creek bed. He was picking berries off a big bush and thought he heard a commotion on the other side. Just as he stood up, a bear's head rose on the other side of the bush. As Wally darted away from the scene, he glanced around to see the bear dashing away in the other direction. Never knew who scared who.

Another episode with an animal was when young Wally chased a small black and white furry animal into his hole. He got a stick and probed around in the hole and had quite a tussle before he finally got him out. You guessed it, a skunk. When he came home proudly carrying the carcass of this animal, Catherine, seeing him from about a hundred yards, yelled to him that if that thing he was carrying was what she thought it was, for him to take all of his clothes off and leave the skunk right there. He proceeded to do this and had to walk, in humiliation, across the prairie the remaining distance to the house to be scrubbed down in a steaming tub of water before his mother would let him in.

I suppose all children remember some of the things they did that got their parents extremely mad, resulting in pretty good spankings. Tom had a prize horse he was raising. It was kept with a rope tied around its neck and attached to a tree so it would not wander off. One day Wally snuck up behind the horse, yelling and giving the horse a hell of a scare. The horse darted, ran across the grass to the length of the rope, which snapped him over on his neck. The horse's neck was not broken, but Tom saw the whole thing. He ran out the door and trounced Wally right in the barnyard. The horse had run through Catherine's flower patch, and as soon as Tom was through with Wally, she started in.

Irrigation ditches were the closest things to swimming pools Wally and his peers had in the dry prairie areas. There was very little natural water. Their one creek produced a memory Wally never forgot. He was swimming with a boy named Sweeney. Sweeney dove under the water and accidentally got his head lodged between two roots of an over-hanging tree. He was not able to dislodge himself in time and drowned. There were several other violent accidents my father remembered; luckily he was not involved in them as a victim.

One day Wally and another friend were running through a barnyard that contained pigs. A big sow evidently became overly protective of her piglets, and thinking Wally and his friend were going to harm them, she started chasing the boys. Just as they got to a fence, Wally jumped over it and his friend tried to do the same. As his friend was in mid-flight, the sow grabbed the calf muscle of his leg and ripped it out. The boy was a cripple for the rest of his life.

Wally once saw his dad rocking in a chair on the front porch as a rattlesnake—which evidently had gotten up on the porch railing—struck out and knocked the straw hat right off his head. When I was in New Mexico and Colorado in 1965, I understood why there were so many snake stories. It was amazing to me that at almost every half-mile of the highway there was a dead snake. My father used to say that, just as my mother told me to be careful of cars when I was a little boy, his mother told him to be careful of snakes. They are almost as prevalent out there as mosquitoes.

He used to say how lonely it would be on Sundays. Wally used to lie on the side of a prairie hill wondering if those same clouds and sky were over the big towns that he had heard of but would probably never see, such as Chicago, New York and San Francisco. Vacations were very simple and inexpensive outings. Once or twice a year Tom would pack up the family and go right straight up into the mountains, where they would camp for two or three weeks, drinking out of the clean pure mountain streams.

When Dad and I were out there in 1965, he commented that a clear running stream was almost a forgotten part of the American landscape. Nonetheless, we did find many of them up in the same mountains where he had camped as a boy; he got a tremendous thrill leaning over and drinking just as he had as a boy. He was a very sentimental man and little things like that could bring tears to his eyes.

It's interesting how little episodes in one's youth are recalled, their memory then passed on to one's offspring. Dad told me that before his family left the west, he was old enough to have gone to one or two school dances with girls. He remembered how horribly embarrassing it was to be riding in a buggy with a girl you were scared to death of anyway and have the horse stop, lift its tail, and do its business right in front of God, you and your girlfriend.

Tom was not content for his family to depend on horse and buggy. He had the first car Pictou saw, a Model T Ford. The miners took great pleasure in ribbing Tom about the car. When he drove it on the muddy road of Pictou, he'd either get stuck or the engine would conk out. One day Tom climbed out and over the hood and reached down to turn the crank. All the while the miners, standing on the planked board walk, jeered and called, "Get a hoss, Tom, get a hoss!"

Eventually the time came when Tom and Catherine decided to leave the west. The way this decision was reached is intriguing. Catherine, being from Milwaukee, had never truly liked the west and the type of life that was led out there. It was a bit raw and crude for a woman who had come from a more civilized type of life. In addition, her in-laws' cruel ostracization of her because she came from a Catholic family made her western life even less pleasant. She had just about had it with the west. They were living in Pictou, Colorado, when events started happening that really iced the cake.

Tom was neither a miner nor a manager. His job was to install equipment and stay long enough so that the miners in charge of the equipment knew how to run and repair it. Tom, Catherine and their children had lived in this town for probably six or seven years. Wally had been about seven when they moved to Pictou and about 14 when his parents decided to leave. There was a big Colorado strike, called the Ludlow Strike, that is written up in labor history books. The miners in Pictou were disgruntled over certain conditions that existed there, and they were out to get anybody that represented management. Tom, to them, represented management, even though he was in no way connected with management. Rumors were flying. One story was that the miners in a town called Ludlow went up on the side of the mountains and opened up on the state militia with Gatling guns. Although this did not happen in Pictou, it typified the violence and high stress level the Chowns were encountering in Pictou.

For several nights in a row, bullets whizzed through the windows of Tom and Catherine's home, and they would all have to hit the deck. This was the straw that broke the camel's back. In the middle of a November night in 1917 they packed what few belongings they could take with them in Tom's car, then took off across the prairie. Wally had a geography book with a map of the United States, nothing close to an Atlas or road map. This rough map was what the family used to guide them all the way back to Milwaukee. They would aim toward some town that was shown on the map, then stop at one farm, then the next, asking for directions. All this was over open prairie or, at best, dirt roads. The traveling Chowns were considered such an oddity that several farmers asked them to stay over for a few days. Wally remembered one family in particular who prevailed on them to stay three or four days and relate some of the experiences they had had along the way. It took a couple of months in the Model T to get from Pictou to Milwaukee.

10

Back East

THE DAYS OF TOM AND CATHERINE, THEIR CHILDREN AND FUTURE PROGENY AS WESTERNERS were over. Even as I wrote down these events from my recollection of my father's words, I realized they might not be totally factual. The exact dates and places are of little concern to me. My intention is to relate some colorful incidents, remembered by my father, from the days when he was a young boy in the western United States. This background of wild, uncorralled youth was, I am sure, the reason why he developed into a most individualistic and imaginative man. He had spent so much time alone, he was forced to see pleasant and entertaining things where others would surely miss them. He never lost his appreciation of simplicity, especially in nature's beauty. And he developed one helluva sense of humor!

I have used Wally's reminiscences as a way to look at the young, middle-aged couple, Thomas and Catherine Chown, and their two children. (Son Walter got a beloved baby sister, Marion, born in East Las Vegas, New Mexico, in 1906.)

All these fanciful memories I have come to believe are true . . . or have a kernel of truth around which maybe a pearl has grown. Think of your own life. Maybe something really funny, or scary, or momentous happened to you and a friend or sibling. Even the next day or month or year later, you may not both retell it exactly the same way. But even many years later you'll probably both agree on the basic core of the event. I think that is what all this is. Surely, experiencing youth in the violence and rawness of early western mining towns would have left an indelible impression on young Wally and Marion. Being three years younger, she may not have absorbed what he did. And the exact same situations would have had totally different effects on Tom and Catherine. Tom's acceptance of that rawboned existence, having been born into it, was assuredly different than Catherine's reaction, coming from back east.

So skedaddle they did. And according to a reference letter for Tom from the Colorado Fuel and Iron Co., they left in November 1917. Wally was about fourteen years old and Marion about eleven or twelve. My saying their days as westerners were over is not totally true. Neither young Walter nor sister Marion nor mother Catherine ever went back to live in Colorado or New Mexico, but Tom did. Before I proceed down the Chown path as easterners, I want to wrap up the Odyssey of Tom and Catherine as best I know it.

The family finally arrived back in Wisconsin. They went to Milwaukee, I'm sure because many of Catherine's Rodden relatives were there. And opportunity was there, not up on the farm in Cascade. Certainly she had had it with rural life and wanted for herself and her children the advantages of a big city. She was still a staunch Roman Catholic, and Marquette, a great Jesuit University, was in Milwaukee. Can you imagine the joy for Catherine to have an extended family again?

The Chowns had most likely never warmed up to her. There was one exception, I would like to think, in Tom's mother, Mary. After all, she remained in that torn picture. I just have a gut feeling that Mary was one wise old woman and may have offered some warmth to her baby boy's wife. But Tom and Catherine never lived close to any family out west, anyway. We have a picture of Catherine with a Red Cross-type nursing group in Walsenburg. I'm sure the photo was taken in front of the Huerfano County Courthouse and is a group of ladies trying to give some health care to the families at the Pictou mine. I'm certain Catherine had female friends. But never living in any one spot very long and having no close family must have been difficult. Her "Memories" poem is very telling . . . and from her heart.

Back in Milwaukee, Catherine got to rejoin the bosom of her Rodden clan. It is possible that she had not seen her mother or father at all during her 15-year western sojourn, although with her access to the Santa Fe Railroad, she may have made several trips back. Wally went to Marquette Academy, then he attended Marquette University for three years. They probably had a normal life for eight or so years in Milwaukee . . . actually, it was hugely normal when compared to bullets flying through their house in Pictou. I hope Tom and Catherine enjoyed those years, because a devastating change came on June 4, 1925. At age 47, Catherine died of "hemorrhagic" small pox. Tom would have been almost 50. They lived at 937 Vliet Street. We have a last picture of her at that address.

Wally used to tell a very poignant story about his mother's death. Small pox is, of course, a highly contagious disease. When it hit Milwaukee in 1925, it must have been considered the plague. Naturally, Catherine and her whole family were quarantined at home—nobody in, nobody out. One of my dad's best friends was Ed Reichert, whom he had met at Marquette. Ed was dating and would later marry Marion Chown. The whole family loved Ed, and he loved them. When Catherine was so sick, obviously dying and very contagious, somebody had to bring food and necessities to the Chowns. That somebody was Ed Reichert. He came every day at great risk to himself to bring supplies. He used to pull himself up to a side window and look in . . . and cry. Wally and Marion would look out at him . . . and cry. They all wanted so badly to help their mother, but they couldn't. Catherine died leaving a distraught husband, son and daughter.

Catherine Rodden Chown was, like her mother-in-law, a remarkable woman. She had been a beautiful young girl with a slightly different role to play than Mary Ellen McGinnis Chown. Hers wasn't as truly a pioneering role. Mary McGinnis would never have had the opportunity to be photographed in that long elegant dress and cape and wearing that plumed black hat. Their backgrounds were different. But both had to be very gutsy, very tough, very adventuresome women. They in many ways were cut from the same cloth. They may not have known it in life, but I'll bet they know it now!

11

Tom's Life After Catherine

THINGS MUST HAVE BEEN DIFFICULT FOR TOM CHOWN AFTER THE DEATH OF HIS WIFE CATHERINE in 1925. He was about 49 years old, had been married to her for 23 years or so, and still had Wally and Marion to care for—or so it seemed. In reality, Wally would be married in 1926, so he was soon out of the nest, and Marion would marry Ed Reichert a couple of years later. That probably left Tom living a pretty lonely life. He had basically the reverse situation in the east that Catherine had had out west—no extended family or long time friends. We know he was a full time combustion engineer at this time in his life, putting in power plants all around the upper Midwest and northeast. We have several letters to him from his employer, the Fuller-Lehigh Company, out of Fullerton, Pennsylvania. The first, dated September 22, 1924, states that he is being hired at a salary of $300 a month plus expenses. His duties were to be "starting up powdered coal fired boilers and putting them into regular operation." The next couple of letters dated in 1926 place him in Cincinnati at the Business Men's Club. We know he was in Allentown, Pennsylvania, the previous year because of a telegram sent to him on June 2, 1925, from his daughter, Marion. It reads: "Mother not expected to live, come home."

A letter in 1931 from Fuller Lehigh Company terminates Tom's employment with them. It praises his seven years with them as "entirely satisfactory" and states they had been "pleased with your initiative and ability to get along with other employees and customers." The reason for his termination is given as "the curtailment of forces we are obliged to make due to lack of work." Look again at that date: 1931. The stock market crash occurred in 1929. The country was in the Great Depression. Tom Chown's life back east was finished. His job prospects were non-existent. He was now a 55-year-old unemployed widower. His two children were both married and had their own lives to lead. So what did he do?

Thomas Wolfe Was Wrong!

Tom moved back to Colorado. He went to LaMar, a small town just inside the Kansas border, and married a woman named Lila Pike, whom he had known many years earlier. From what we can gather, they hand-built the "Rock House" pictured in Plate 32, in the photographs following this chapter. The place is extremely remote and primitive, even now. Barbara and I visited it in 1999 with the permission and guidance of its current owner, David Frank. About thirty miles south of LaMar, it is located in desolate, flat, eastern Colorado cow and wheat country. David Frank has been there almost his whole life and is a true cowboy and a true gentleman. He said his father remembered Tom Chown but had died several years earlier. He said his father described "old Tom" as a friendly man who could build or fix anything. He thought Tom had been with the Santa Fe, and that's where he got the wooden beams (railroad ties) to use as rafters for his hand-built rock house. The horse corral is all rock, wholly constructed by Tom. (These rock ruins are almost considered shrines now, and are protected by the state of Colorado.)

We have photos of my parents, Peg and Wally, visiting Tom and Lila in that barren spot in 1941. My father told me years later he was appalled at the primitive conditions in which his father and Lila were living: no electricity, no indoor toilet—very rough. Apparently, however, that was their choice.

A very indelicate—but, according to my father, true—story of how tough the people had to be out there involved Lila's father. He was in his 80s and lived about a mile away, but within eyesight of Tom and Lila. One winter day he fell down while slopping his hogs. One of them attacked him and tore open his scrotum. He blacked out, but awoke with his dog standing on his chest keeping the hog at bay. He crawled into his house and sewed himself up with burlap string. Tom and Lila found him three days later. He lived several more years . . . tough guy!

According to my father, Tom had arrived in LaMar in 1931 with a "pretty good chunk" of savings, which he deposited in a local bank. He lost it all in the famous "Bank Holiday" part of the depression. Then to add to his misery, the dust storms killed the cattle and turkeys he had raised. On April 11, 1944, the same dust storms killed Tom. My father said the last few years of Tom's life he had a constant cough. Of course, he was a smoker, but added to that was the constant dust . . . everywhere—even through closed doors and windows. Get yourself a book on the Dust Bowl Years and look at the pictures. That was Tom and Lila. (We know Lila lived past age 83 from a letter we got from her in 1972).

Tom Chown died in what must have been pretty bleak conditions, following a decade or more of the same. Nonetheless, every comment I have heard about him has attested to his spunk. My dad said one time Tom and Lila were driving down a country road out there and a carload of young toughs kept passing and slowing down . . . playing leap frog. Tom finally had enough. He passed them one last time and stopped in the middle of the road. They couldn't get around him on either side. He got out of the car with a ball-peen hammer and approached them. Nobody got out of the offending car. So Tom simply went all around the car making nice circular little dents in every fender with his hammer. That took care of that problem.

Another story involved Tom and a friend hunting geese nearby at a place called Flyway Reservoir (probably Martin Reservoir). The geese were too high to reach with an ordinary shotgun, so they somehow built a long-barreled "cannon" and mounted it on a raft out in the lake. Here came the geese . . . The trigger was pulled on the cannon: Boom! Down went the raft!

In spite of hard times, Tom Chown seemed to display a good humor to the end. Although he basically must have "died broke"—he didn't own a suit and was buried in one of Walter's—his last sentence was a joke. Supposedly a friend was sitting by his deathbed in the LaMar hospital when Tom noticed his friend.

"I've been admiring your coat, Mike," Tom said, "especially the top button. Do you like it, too?"

"Yes, Tom, I like the button," Mike replied.

"Do you want to keep it?" Tom asked.

"Yes, Tom," his puzzled friend replied.

Whereupon Tom reached out his hand, ripped off the button and handed it to Mike. "Here Mike . . . it's yours!"

And then he died.

An interesting footnote to Tom's death on April 11, 1944, is his certificate of baptism to Catholicism on April 10 by the priest from St. Francis DeSales Church in LaMar. With his own family's anti-Catholic leaning, this must have been a big step. Maybe he was buying a little insurance . . . just in case. Or maybe it reflected his love for Catherine.

Thomas Albert Chown I is my namesake. I am, thus, Thomas Albert Chown II. Our lives overlapped by almost exactly one year. I was born April 23, 1943, and he died April 11, 1944. He never laid eyes on me, but if he had I would have been too young to remember anyway. He did, however, visit his daughter, Marion, and her family in Richmond, Minnesota. We have two good pictures from that occasion. There is one of him with his Reichert grandchildren. I believe, at least, Tom Reichert remembers him, and maybe Ed and Wally Reichert do too. (By the way, Wally Reichert's middle name is Chown—named after his uncle, my father) The other picture is of Tom Chown in bib overalls with a string of fish.

Aunt Marion was very special to me, and she and my dad—her brother, Wally—were able to visit several times in their later years. As we will see, Wally died in 1969. What memories they shared together of their "wild west" youth and early Milwaukee years! They are both "up yonder" somewhere right now looking down approvingly on all of us.

At this juncture I will let Tom Reichert continue his own way down the Chown path as it merges into the Reichert family tree. It, of course, flows from Tom and Catherine Chown, through their daughter, Marion, who became a Reichert upon her marriage in 1928 to Edward Reichert, a wonderful man who helped my Aunt Marion raise four terrific children. All four—Thomas George (born 1929), Edward Marion (1930), Walter Chown (1932) and the baby girl, Mary Alice Kathryn (1938)—were on hand for Ed and Marion's Golden Wedding Anniversary in 1978. Marion Chown Reichert passed away on December 4, 1980, at the age of 74.

One last comment on Tom and Catherine Chown: none of us can say exactly what they were like as people. We can—and, in fact, we have—surmised a lot just by big events we know made up their lives. I truly believe the best criteria of how well a couple "ran the race" is not their money or station in life. I think their value can most clearly be seen in the kind of children they raised. It would appear Tom and Catherine had more than their share of hardship, but oh, what children they raised! My father was by far the finest, most interesting, best man I ever met. I know the Reicherts feel the same about their mother, Marion. That speaks volumes for Tom and Catherine.

PLATE 23. RODDEN/CHOWN FAMILY.

Top: A Rodden/Chown family gathering photographed around 1920, when Catherine was back in the bosom of her family. She is in the middle of the photograph, between two women wearing pearls. Tom and son Wally are standing in the back row, far right; daughter Marion is in the front row, far left.

Bottom: Wally and Marion with their dad, Tom. This photo was probably taken between 1920 and '25.

PLATE 24. WALTER C. CHOWN I.

Top: Wally in 1923, at a lumber camp in Montana.

Above, right: Wally and friend with "flivver" in 1925. Wally was called Chong because he named his band "Chong's Melody Boys," after a hot song of the time by that name.

Left: Walter, probably at his graduation from Marquette Academy in Milwaukee, Wisconsin, in 1921, when he was 18.

PLATE 25. THE AUTHOR'S MOTHER, MARGARET E. CHOWN, a.k.a. Peggy, at 20. Like the following photo of Walter, this is probably a wedding photo, taken in 1926.

PLATE 26. THE AUTHOR'S FATHER, WALTER C. CHOWN I AT 23. This is probably a wedding photo, taken in 1926. He signed it, "To my little Thornrose." She remained his little thornrose forever.

PLATE 27. THE AUTHOR'S PARENTS, Margaret E. "Peggy" Mathews and
Walter C. Chown. This photo was taken in 1925, prior to their marriage.
On the back is written, "1st picture ever taken of us." They were beautiful.

Sweet Bird of Youth

Plate 28. Peggy, Walter and Tom.

Top left: Wedding photo of Peggy and Wally in 1926 in Milwaukee—the start of a terrific 43-year run.

Top right: The honeymoon—after the wedding in Milwaukee or after their elopement in Iowa?

Bottom left: Tom and Wally enjoying a pleasant father/son activity, probably around 1925.

Bottom right: Wally clowning around with friends in Omaha, 1932.

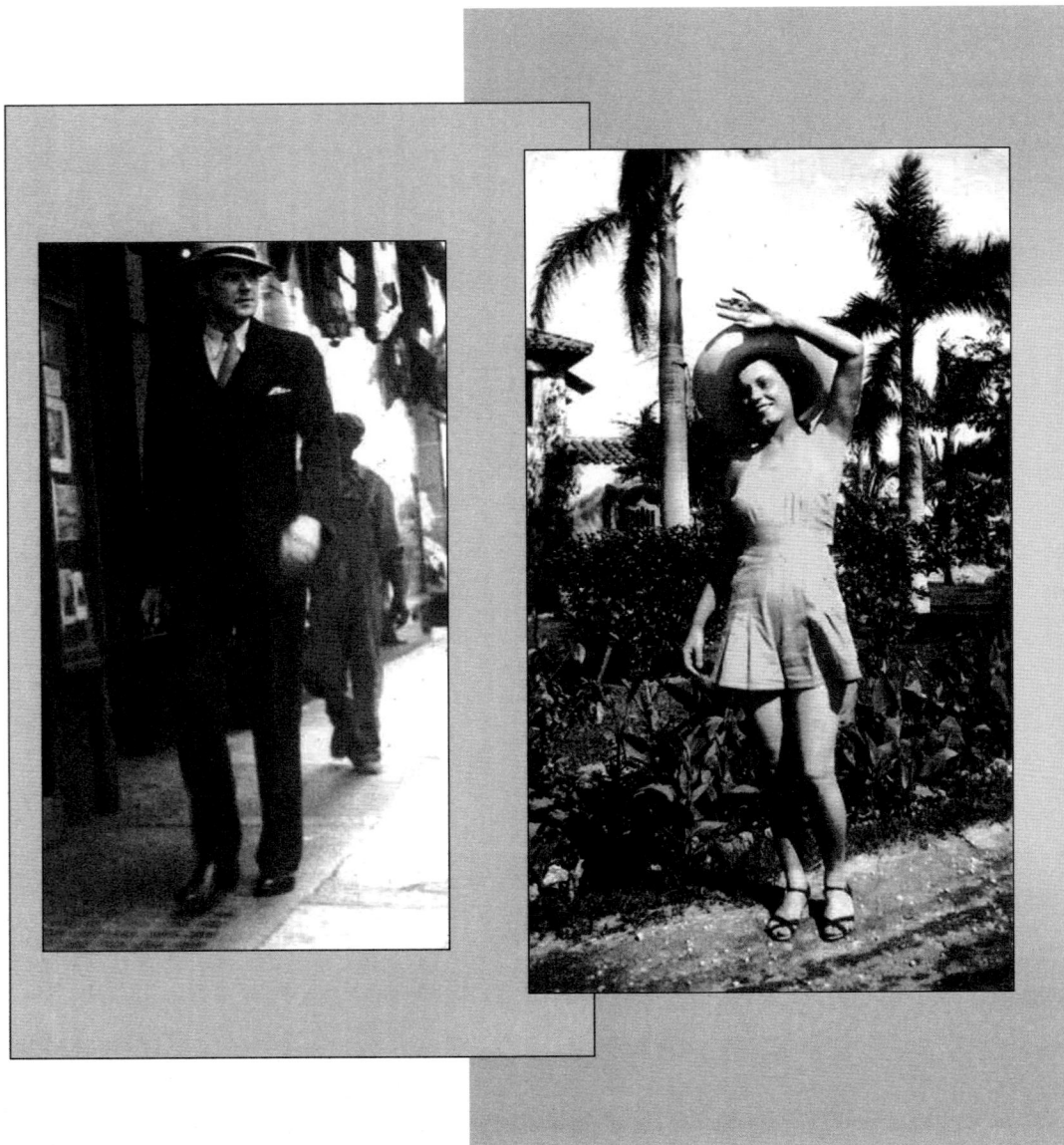

PLATE 29. WALTER AND PEGGY IN THE 1930S.

Left: Wally Chown in St. Louis, in 1935; he was 32.

Right: Peggy Chown as a "glamour girl" in Coral Gables, Florida, in 1930; she was 24.

PLATE 30.
LIFE BEFORE WALLY: LOOKING BACK AT PEGGY.

Left: Sophia Mathews and little daughter, Margaret Emily (Peggy). The photo was probably taken around 1910, when Peggy was four. This is a second torn picture. Peggy is holding the hand of her father, Charles Mathews. When he abandoned his wife and child, he was cut out of the picture . . . just as he had cut himself out of their lives.

Below: Peggy and Sophia; Peggy was about 16.

PEG, ALONG THE PATH OF LIFE

PLATE 31. PEG BEFORE AND AFTER WALLY.

Top left: First Communion, age 10, at St. Johns, Worcester, Massachusetts, 1916.

Top right: Perhaps at an elementary school graduation.

Bottom left: At high school graduation; Peggy was Valedictorian and commencement speaker in 1925 at High School of Commerce.

Bottom right: Around 1990, one of the last photos taken of Peggy, here with her son, Tom, the author of this book. She died in 2000 at age 94.

PLATE 32. COLORADO REVISITED.

Top: The rock house build south of LaMar by Tom I, c. 1931.

Above, left: Wally I in front of one day's bag of jack rabbits and birds at the rock house in 1941.

Center right: On the same day, Tom I and wife Lila Pike.

Bottom, right: Peg with greyhound and a gun she likely never used.

REICHERT WEDDING AND GOLDEN ANNIVERSARY

PLATE 33. REICHERT WEDDING AND GOLDEN ANNIVERSARY. Marion Chown wed Edward Reichert July 28, 1928. They celebrated their golden anniversary on July 28, 1978.

PLATE 34. THE REICHERT FAMILY.

Above: Reichert clan in 1954: seated, left to right: Edward, daughter Mary Alice, Marion. Sons and daughters-in-law are standing, left to right: Wally, Milly, Bud, Virginia, Tom.

Left: Grandpa Tom Chown visited the Reicherts in Richmond, Minnesota, in 1939; here he stands with his Reichert grandsons, left to right: Eddie, Tom and Wally, on Tom's 10th birthday.

CHOWNS AND REICHERTS

PLATE 35. CHOWNS AND REICHERTS.

Above: the last good photo of sister and brother, Marion and Wally. It was taken at the Reicherts' lake house in Richmond, Minnesota, in 1963. Both had come a long way since their coal mine days!

Right, left to right: Wally Reichert, Tom II and Wally Chown and Reicherts Ed, Ed Jr. (Bud) and Tom.

12

Walter the First

The next male Chown down the line is, of course, Tom and Catherine's son, Walter. We discussed his Colorado boyhood as part of Tom and Catherine's story. Now we look at Walter's teen years to young manhood in Milwaukee, beginning in 1917, when he was fourteen. This period came to a natural end with the death of his mother in 1925, followed quickly by his marriage to Margaret in 1926.

The 1970 narrative I wrote when I was 27 years old is invaluable now, for my "memory gland" worked much better then than it does now at 61. There may be a few inaccuracies and contradictions here, when measured against what we have found out since 1970, but this earlier version is the freshest recall I'll ever have of my dad.

After the long trip across the country to Milwaukee, Wally found himself at about age fourteen in the town where his mother's family resided. Wally recalled several unusual incidents as a boy coming from out west where things were not quite as refined as they were in an eastern city—eastern as far as he was concerned. He had the appearances of a cowboy He wore boots and was inclined to fight at a drop of a hat, thinking it was more sport than anything else. He went out for football at the Marquette Academy (probably being the equivalent to a freshman in high school when he began), but he had never played football. All he knew was that he was supposed to knock the fellow down. Well, the first time he got a chance, he tackled the guy with the ball. When the fellow tried to get up, Wally knocked him down again. The guy got mad, and the new kid from Colorado overwhelmed him . . . wouldn't let him off the ground. The coach finally came over and explained to Wally that after you tackled a man he was allowed to get up for the next play.

Wally was a pretty good athlete. When he was in school he played football, baseball and track. I have a picture around the house of what he referred to as "the shinny team," just a bunch of friends that used to hit a can with a stick, up and down the street, but he took sports seriously a little later, seriously enough to become, as I mentioned before, the heavyweight boxing champion of Marquette Academy. He also played football, as left end, for Marquette. On Sundays he played football under the assumed name of Murphy for a local semi-pro team that would travel from Marquette to Green Bay and all the different little towns around that part of Wisconsin. Finally the Marquette people found out that he was playing semi-pro ball and disqualified him from any further playing. Wally had gotten a letter from Knute Rockne, the famous Notre Dame coach, asking him to come down to talk with him about the possibility of playing with Notre Dame. He never went down. He had to work so hard in those years that anything athletic he did was purely for fun, and only now and then. Practices were almost non-existent; they just played their games. I have a picture of him on the track team. He was a high-jumper and jumped 5'11". (It is ironic that I also was a high-jumper and my best effort was also 5'11".)

Wally remarked once that he had gone to Chicago to participate in the Stagg Relays, named after Alonzo Stagg, the famous coach who had been, I believe, at the University of Chicago. Stagg was a famous football and track coach, and Wally recalled that there were athletes from all over the country at the relays. He and his teammates were decent athletes, but they got whipped substantially in almost every event. The only specific thing Wally remembered about it was the dormitories where the other athletes were sleeping. He and a friend snuck in late at night and painted faces on the soles of their feet hanging over the end of the cots. Imagine probably fifty guys waking up in the morning with smiles on their feet.

As I have said, Wally's mother's family, the Roddens, came from Cascade, Wisconsin. Her Irish father, Mike, had actually walked all the way from Pennsylvania to Cascade, after a stint working on the Erie Canal. The days of emigrating from Ireland to escape the potato famine must have seemed far behind him as he and his wife, Mary, proceeded to raise sixteen children—one of them, Wally's mother, Catherine. Mike was reputed to have been quite a fist fighter, although he was not a big man.

Wally spoke often about summer journeys up to Cascade with his family, swimming in Lake Allen, a local lake up there, with several different cousins, uncles, and other relatives. He also recalled a winter trip to Cascade. He claimed it got so cold that he actually heard nails firing out of the contracting wood in the house. The nails were squeezed out with such a velocity that they would be found stuck in trees the following day. (That is another bit of information that I, as a kid, never knew whether to believe. Wouldn't the whole damned house fall down after several cold winters?)

The idea of Wally's being the heavyweight champ of Marquette Academy was another concept I, as his son, never really accepted. I was sure the old man was just pulling my leg again, but darned if he didn't write to an old priest he knew, asking him to look up an account of him in the academy yearbook. There it was, an article about Wally winning the heavyweight boxing championship. It made a believer out of me, but I've lost that letter . . . I did see it, though! Wally had many good friends when he was in Marquette. Ed Reichert and Milo Larson were two of the best. When Ed came courting Marion, the friendship took on a new dimension. Wally, being a big brother, was naturally protective of his little sister and just as obnoxious as he could be, making life miserable for Ed and Marion during their courtship. More than once when Ed came over to visit Marion, Wally would come into the room where they were sitting on the sofa, not say a word, and line up about a dozen fat apples. Then he would very slowly, while staring at them, eat the first apple. After he had finished that he would very slowly pick up the second apple and start nibbling on it. Can you imagine the frustration that Ed and Marion must have felt waiting for her brother to go through a dozen apples before they could have any privacy?

The other friend, Milo Larson, evidently was just as ornery as Wally. He was a student in medical school, and he used to get parts from human cadavers and give them to my father to pull pranks with. One time Wally had a part-time job with an insurance firm. He was to go out and collect the weekly premiums from people and hand in what he had collected in an envelope at the end of each day. At the end of one day he waited patiently in line, finally stepping up to the cashier's window. He handed her the envelope, but instead of the receipts from that day's collection, the envelope contained a human little finger. He had gotten about five feet away from the window when he heard a blood-curdling shriek. The poor gal who had taken the envelope had become completely hysterical. The boss finally came out, calmed her down . . . and fired Wally.

Another time Milo filched a hand. He and Wally spied a convertible parked on a downtown street, walked up to it and nonchalantly placed the hand on the front seat. Imagine what you would think if you came out after an afternoon of shopping, hopped into your convertible, looked down and saw a severed hand. They really had a devilish sense of humor. Maybe "sicko" is a more apt description.

When Wally later worked (full-time) at another insurance firm, he and another fellow would sit in the office for hours during the afternoon heating pennies until they became white hot and dropping them onto the sidewalk below. People coming by, seeing a penny lying there, would bend over to pick it up. They let go real fast. (Oddly enough, Wally never really made it in the insurance business.)

Wally and Ed Reichert always had a great mutual appreciation of each other. Ed enjoyed telling about the time he and Wally rode all the way across town to get to a dance. This was in the middle of a Milwaukee winter, and both young men were shivering as they left the dance. It was probably about one or two in the morning and the temperature outside about 20° below 0 when they got on the streetcar, heading back to their homes. Both of them, being as poor as church mice, were wearing very thin, threadbare pants. All of a sudden Wally slapped his hands right over the top of Ed's leg and tore the one pant leg right off of him. There he was in that severe cold with his bare leg hanging out. The only thing he could do was laugh.

Walter Chown was a real alive type of fellow. He had more pizazz to him than most other men I have known. He organized a group called Chong's Melody Boys. It would have been Chown's Melody Boys, but there was a current hit song called "Chong," and they wanted to capitalize on the name. They had three or four fellows in the band, in addition to Wally. He played the banjo just enough to make noise. Anyone who ever singled him out and listened to him would have realized Wally was playing no tune at all. Essentially he was the organizer, setting up dates at different dances all across the city, for his group to play. He would take half of the payment and give the rest of it to the other three fellows. They had great times. I kept one of his small banjos—a mandolin-type of instrument—for years, but have since given it to my son, Wally II.

On a hazing day at Wally's college fraternity at Marquette, he and a friend, as active members, took three pledges out in the country. The pledges were freshmen football players— very large people. Going far out into rural Wisconsin, the two "brothers" planned to leave the poor pledges out there to fend for themselves. When they got to their destination, the pledges—sitting in the back seat in very tight quarters—inhaled and expanded their chests and shoulders. Wally and his friend could not budge them from the car. The only thing they could do was get back into the car and drive all the way back to Milwaukee, admitting defeat.

In those days there were some great fights between the freshmen and sophomore classes trying to climb up a greased pole. Apparently it got pretty brutal, with a lot of cuts and broken bones. Universities have long since outlawed this type of behavior in the fraternities.

Wally thought of himself as quite a ladies' man, but he recalled with humor that it once got him into trouble. He loved to ice skate, and one day on a pond he was showing off his most daring tricks to try to catch the eye of a particular pretty miss who was also skating nearby. He got up to full speed, then turned to see if she was looking . . . and ran smack into a low bridge, knocking himself out, cold as a mackerel. What a way to impress a girl.

When Wally's mother died, his father didn't have much money, so Wally had to work for whatever he got. A variety of jobs served that purpose. For a while he worked for a bakery, driving a delivery truck full of baked goods all over the city in the day time and working in the factory at night, producing the bread. For the rest of his life he had a great aversion to any type of factory work, largely based on that brief experience. He was in charge of keeping the bread assembly belt going. The baked bread would come out onto a belt that started at the top of the ceiling and work its way, zig-zagging, down the entire wall, then go up to the next wall and do the same thing. This was engineered to take a certain amount of time for the bread to cool. It would then arrive at the appropriate area for packaging. Wally's job was to keep the thing running at the proper speed, so that each loaf of bread could be wrapped at just the right moment. One particular night, Wally did something to the machine and it stopped working correctly . . . but he couldn't get it to shut off. Bread was hitting the floor at the packaging area and piling higher and higher and higher as Wally worked furiously to shut off the assembly belt. Finally he got it stopped, but all the bread was too dirty to be saved. (This sounds like the old I Love Lucy skit, with Lucy and Ethel eating candy coming too fast on the assembly belt.) That probably cost him his job.

Another job he had was sitting up nights with a priest who had a disease. I can't think of the name of it, but I believe it was Parkinson's disease or Hodgkin's disease, with which one starts slowly shaking and, if not attended, eventually almost shakes to death. This was very difficult for young Wally, because he had to stay awake after going to school all day, then working another job and, finally, showing up to sit all night with the priest. Wally's endurance finally ran out, and he had the equivalent of a nervous breakdown. After only several weeks in a hospital for rest, he was back on the old grind again.

Once Wally got a job that sounded mysterious. He was to drive a truck from Milwaukee to Chicago, but was never told the contents of the truck. After he had made the run once he was told the merchandise was bootleg liquor. That was during the days of Prohibition, and rum running, as it was called, was a lucrative line of work. Only one little problem: the previous two drivers on that route had been killed. As soon as Wally discovered this bit of information, he gave up the job. Bootlegging must have been quite a thing. Wally recalled that at almost every dance he ever attended in Milwaukee, there would always be one or two fellows standing outside the door with big, heavy, long, droopy overcoats on. If you asked correctly, out of the deep pockets would come pint flasks of liquor, for sale at the proper price.

A Year of Adventure

Wally and his friend Dick Porth took off after they had graduated from Marquette Academy and went out to Kansas where the wheat was ripening. They followed it all the way around the country and helped harvest the wheat until they found themselves in Montana. There they signed on with a lumber company and were lumberjacks throughout the following year. He was a teamster, in that he had had experience with horses when he was out west and could handle a team. Dick was an actual lumberjack who would work up in the mountains sawing down the trees. The downed trees would be chained together and dragged down the hill by horses. My father operated one of these teams of horses. After working for quite awhile in the lumber camp, Wally and Dick hit Fargo, North Dakota, and spent some time there in the poker games. Poor Dick lost every cent he had made over the previous year in the poker games. That taught Wally a lesson about gambling that lasted the rest of his life.

There was a funny (though indelicate) story about Dick Porth, which happened on their way back. Naturally a couple of young men like that didn't have money for first-class transportation, so they just hopped rides on freight trains. When they would have to go to the bathroom, they would place themselves between two railroad cars, feet against one and back against another, with their pants down around their ankles. That seemed to be a good way to go to the bathroom with out fouling up their own quarters inside the train. On one occasion Dick was evidently wedged between two of the cars in that position. The train, unfortunately, went around a bend in the tracks, which naturally opened up the outside expanse between the two cars. Dick flew out with his bare fanny hanging out and hit the cinders in that position. My father, noticing that he had not come back for a while, looked down the track and saw him lying way back there in utter agony. Wally jumped off the train and spent approximately the next three or four hours picking cinders out of Dick's behind. Oh, the humility of it all!

When Wally finally got back to Milwaukee, he had a full beard. He had not shaved during the entire period, and when he got to the front door of his house, Marion didn't recognize him.

Wally Woos Peggy

Wally had met Miss Margaret Emily Mathews of Worcester, Massachusetts, while he was in college at Marquette. It didn't take very long for him to decide she was the gal for him. Being the aggressive sort of person he was, he saw no particular reason in wasting time. He had met Peg when he and a friend of his, Charlie Harding, were fixing a flat tire on Charlie's car. Peg, a freshman at Marquette University, was walking down the street with a friend. The four young people struck up a conversation, and when the tire was fixed they all hopped into the car to go get a soda at the local drug store. Wally was in the back seat with Peg's friend, and Peggy was in the front seat with Charlie. When they got to the soda shop Wally grabbed Charlie aside and told him that whether he liked it or not, they were switching dates. Wally was a fairly dominate figure and not to be argued with. So that is what happened.

Peg and Wally started dating then and had a brief period of time trying to outsmart each other. Peg had been quite popular back in Massachusetts. Her mother had sent her out to Marquette University to go to college where her aunt Mae lived and worked as a registered nurse. Wally was supposed to be an all-American boy, a real whiz-bang. Naturally, any woman would jump at the opportunity to be seen in the company of the handsome, charming, debonair and suave Walter C. Chown. Well, my mother gave him sort of a cold shoulder for a while so he decided to play on her sympathies.

Once—I believe it was when he was in the hospital with pure exhaustion from the job load he was carrying—he put a note on her bulletin board to come and see him because he was in the absolute worst of health. She totally ignored him for several days, which about drove him nuts. When he got out of the hospital they ironed that out, evidently well enough that they ran off to Iowa and got married. This was in 1926. They actually had two weddings because Peg's mother was so upset over their not having a regular wedding in a church. Their second wedding ceremony was in a church. I am a little sketchy on the exact particulars of their courtship, other than to know she had been engaged to Frank Hasset back in Massachusetts until Wally took full control of the situation, ending the romance with Frank in its tracks.

Because of the lack of money, Wally dropped out of school once he was a married man, anxious to begin carving his niche in the world. Those were the days when jobs were hard to come by. One day he was shooting pool with a friend when another friend came by. The friend, who was a priest, said he had heard of a sales job with the Holproof Hosiery Company, selling hosiery; he wondered if Wally would be interested. He was. That job started a career in the Hosiery and Foundation Garment Industry, in which he remained for the rest of his life.

Those memories are the sum of what I wrote in 1970 as a young man about my father, Wally Chown, when he, himself, was a young man. Sounds fanciful doesn't it? Do you think he really got a letter from Knute Rockne? I never saw that letter; he said he threw it away years earlier, not attaching any importance to it. As I said, I did see the letter from Marquette verifying the boxing title, but I have no idea what happened to it. My own opinion: it is all true. Wally had a terrific imagination and was an extraordinarily colorful guy. He could describe a cow patty and have you believing it was an exquisite piece of Godiva chocolate. He could enliven stories of his exploits and observations and leave you certain you had been there yourself. But I have three reasons for believing everything he said. One, he never lied . . . about anything (though he did embellish). Two, those friends who actually witnessed many of Wally's stories backed them up. Three, the things I actually witnessed about him in my life were as zany as what he professed about his early life.

With the warning of "let the reader beware"—which is certainly neither imprimatur nor disclaimer—I invite the reader to again follow my 1970 memories of Walter Chown . . . as a young salesman from 1925 to 1960.

Birth of a Salesman

The job with Holproof Hosiery was a windfall for my father. He had been looking for a job, scraping along on whatever money he could make from odd jobs and, all of a sudden, he was getting $100 a week to sell hosiery. This seemed like the real pot of gold to him, and as many young men would do, he abused it. He would take two or three of his fraternity brothers out of town with him and wine them and dine them and treat the whole job just like a vacation, never worrying too much about whether he sold anything. Finally his boss came in one day and relieved him from both his duties and his $100 a week.

Wally pretty well panicked at that point and got a job in a factory again. This was some type of a manufacturing plant, and it taught him, once and for all, that he wanted no part of factory work in any way. He couldn't believe the lack of imagination necessary in that kind of job. He said he lasted about a week of standing in front of a machine and, every three seconds, turning a certain bolt three turns to the left and stomping his foot on a peddle and tightening a screw with his right hand. It was a type of job that his imagination just wouldn't work under. He started looking for another job and had one of his first bouts with bad feet. He had to have the first of four operations and, having absolutely no money, the only place to go was the County Hospital. He remembered being extremely miserable after the operation, lying in a ward full of all types of derelicts. An old man in the bed beside him just complained, complained, complained, all day long. Every time the man's wife would come and try to cheer him up, he would jump all over her and chew her out for something. Wally claimed he was the most cantankerous person who ever lived. All of a sudden, after about a week of this, the man got very mad at somebody and decided to get out of bed and do something about it. In one convulsive effort, he just crumpled up and died right on the floor. Wally said this was one of the only men he had ever seen or heard of dying and feeling a little bit tickled about it.

When Wally was at the absolute depths of depression, his old boss from Holproof Hosiery—the one who had fired him for goofing off on the job—came into the county hospital to visit him. After seeing how absolutely down and out Wally was, the man inquired if he had learned his lesson and asked if he wanted his old job back. Wally jumped at the opportunity. I am not sure how long he worked for Holproof Hosiery, but he was always very grateful to this man, who had bailed him out when he really did need it.

13

Ol'-Time Travelin' Man

His early days on the road as a traveling salesman are almost impossible to comprehend today. Most contemporary salesmen are given a little pie-shaped territory in one city or one state. Wally—still with Holproof Hosiery, I believe—had as a territory everything west of the Mississippi from Canada to Mexico. He would be gone for extremely long stretches at a time, a month or six weeks sometimes. During these periods he had a lot of interesting and amusing encounters. The towns he covered in Arkansas, Texas and the rest of the southwestern United States are so far-flung that the job involved his working all day with a buyer in one store, eating dinner, and then driving almost all night to get to the next town, which might be 200 or 300 miles away. He'd get a little bit of sleep before the store would open, then there he would be to meet the buyer for another day of work. Days and nights must have seemed to run together as he repeated the pattern again and again. His capacity for work was something to behold.

He was driving late one night on a winding road in Arkansas. He came to a hairpin turn in the road and just completely missed it, running right off the road, through an old fence and down into a pasture. Because it was so late at night and he did not know where he was, he figured the best thing to do was to stay there. Minutes after his car had come to a stop—and seconds after his decision to stay put—he heard two thundering collisions on the door beside his driver's seat. It was raining and pitch black, and he had no idea what could have crashed into his door. That further cemented his resolve not to move but to sleep there all night. When he awoke in the morning on a bright, sunny day, he stepped out of the car to look at the door. There were two perfect imprints of the hooves of a mule that had kicked his car. Evidently his car had rolled off the road and come crashing down right behind the mule who, frightened, did what scared mules do: he kicked.

One unpleasant experience Wally had was in St. Joseph, Missouri, sometime in the 1920s or '30s. He had come in on the train and had gotten a hotel room nearby. As he was checking into his room, he heard a commotion going on outside. Looking out the window, he saw a group of men hanging a Negro man from a pole in a gas station. As the poor man was dying, the whites went into the gas station and got all the sharp weapons—knives, ice picks, screwdrivers—they could find. They came back out and completely mutilated the Negro's body before dousing him with gasoline and burning him. On that day, Wally Chown said, he was more ashamed of being a human being than at any other time in his life. (I guess things hadn't changed much since LaJunta in 1902, except that the ring leader was most decidedly not a Chown.)

In those days most salesmen would work a circuit. They would leave one town and go to the next, usually riding together on a train, although some drove cars. Whatever conveyance they used, they would most likely stay in the same rooming house or small hotel, work that town all day, and go on to the next one. They might be together for a week or two. Some would be pot and dish salesmen and others, hardware salesmen and salesmen of all kinds of products. During the winter, some of these early hotels were unbearably cold, with the only heat coming from a pot belly stove in the lobby. During the night, after piling on all the blankets and all the clothes they had available, most of the patrons would finally give up and come down to the lobby and sit by the pot belly stove. That's where Wally heard some of the damnedest stories and tales and jokes that he had ever heard in his life.

All the salesmen had different remedies for the problematic conditions of the time. The early automobiles were almost as much as a hindrance as help. According to Wally, you had to expect to change a tire approximately every hundred miles or so. Another winter problem was frozen windshields. Everybody had a specific remedy for that. Some would take a raw potato and rub it over the windshield inside and out. They believed that the potato had some type of anti-freezing quality to it. Others would have a candle mounted on the dashboard. The heat from it would burn a little hole in the ice, just enough to peer out.

One day Wally came to a traffic signal in some little town and, having the green light, drove into the intersection, just as a dude in a new-fangled car ran the red light on his side and right into Wally. The fellow in the brand new car jumped out, accusing Wally of being at fault, acting as though there was no way my father could pin anything on him. Wally reached in his glove compartment and pulled out a part of his car that had been knocked off a couple of weeks earlier in another accident. I can't remember what it was called, but it was the part out on the end of the hood that was some type of meter. Nonchalantly, Wally got out of the car, paying little attention to the fellow who was really cussing him out. Casually Wally tossed the broken part down on the pavement beside his car. A cop who had seen the accident came up and, not only charged the other fellow with the damage on Wally's car, but also for the part lying beside the car, assuming it had been knocked off in the accident. The guy was pretty honked off.

This was not the first time Wally had put one over on a policeman. One night when Wally and Peg were dating in college, they were parked in some lover's lane when a one-armed cop came up on a motorcycle. He wrote a ticket and gave it to Wally, but as he turned to leave, he discovered that his cycle was lying on its side. After repeated efforts, he realized he could not lift it. Finally he came back and asked Wally to help him lift his cycle. Wally agreed to help . . . if the cop would tear up the ticket—an offer the cop could not refuse; he had no other choice.

Wally always had colorful friends. One in those early days was Barnie Meshott, a Venetian-blind salesman. Wally claimed every time they were in the same town and staying together, Barnie would tear the Venetian blind in the hotel room just enough for the hotel to have to replace it. I guess he figured this had an indirect effect on upping his business. In Rockford, Illinois, one time Wally and Barnie were walking down the street when they saw a couple of fellows throwing a ball back and forth in front of a barber shop. Wally walked up behind one of them and signaled to the other to throw the ball to him over the head of the first one. The fellow did this and Wally caught it. All four of them started throwing the ball, whereupon either Barnie or Wally winged it right through the barber's pole outside the store. Not knowing what would happen, Wally and Barnie took off. The barber ran out of the store and whistled for a policeman, who came quickly, giving chase with the barber, up and down the downtown streets, in and out of the buildings, and right through the lobby and restaurant of the hotel nearby. Finally, after hiding in the kitchen of the restaurant for an hour or two, Wally and Barnie figured they had lost this policeman. They came back to the car, and Wally stepped off the sidewalk to the driver's side. There, lying alongside ther running board of the car, was the policeman, calmly waiting for them to come back . . . and also waiting to be paid for the barber's pole.

More Chicanery

Wally always believed in trying to please the boss. Once he was at a formal dinner at a fancy hotel with the president of Holproof Hosiery. They happened to go to the restroom at the same time, and while they were there, the president of the company mentioned that he really liked a particular ornate mirror that was on the wall of the restroom. When his boss went back to the banquet, Wally figured this was his chance to get in good with him. He unbolted the mirror from the wall with a screwdriver, took it up to his room and called room service. When a young man came up asking if he needed help, Wally said he would like this antique mirror he had just purchased to be wrapped and put in his car. The young porter, having no idea where the mirror came from, procured some wrapping paper from the hotel, wrapped the mirror and carried it out to Wally's car. When Wally gave the mirror to his boss, both of them were gleeful. Who says crime doesn't pay?

My father had another great friend, Huey Fox, whom I met several times. Huey and Wally were great party lovers. Huey had been in the corset business for umpteen years and was somewhat older than Wally. One time Huey had been commiserating with a friend over quite a few bottles of firewater. After they both were sufficiently drunk, Huey got to thinking of his poor sister, whom he had not seen for years, out in California. He decided to get on a plane and fly out there. When he finally sobered up he was high in the air somewhere over Kansas. Suddenly realizing he was deathly afraid of flying, he deplaned right away at the next stop. When he opened his suitcase in the hotel in that particular town, he found that he had packed nothing but neckties.

Thinking of that trip reminds me of Wally's taking a similar one. Once when he was still living in Milwaukee, he had to cross Lake Michigan on the Milwaukee Clipper, a ferry boat going over to a town on the opposite shore. He and Peggy had thrown a big party the night before, either a birthday or anniversary or something. Their friends had taken Wally down to the boat dock early the next morning to get on the Milwaukee Clipper and depart. He got into his berth and lay down on his bed. About half way across the lake he fell asleep, completely missed the stop on the other side, and woke up coming back. Can you imagine the embarrassment in having to buy another ticket and start off on your third leg across Lake Michigan?

Some time in the mid 1930s, Wally and Peggy moved to Columbus, Ohio. They adopted an infant girl, Beth, in August of 1938. Peg gave birth to me five years later. When WWII came my father's company, then Kops Bros., Inc., temporarily shut down their regular production of women's "foundation garments," switching almost entirely to producing the material used for parachutes in the war effort. That fact plus Beth's asthma led them to decide to move to Florida. That was about 1944.

Brief Floridians

For two years our family lived in a little cottage on the beach in Indian Rocks, Florida. Wally received full pay for coming north about three or four weeks during each of those two years. It was paradise for a young family to have nothing to do but fish and swim and enjoy the Florida sunshine. Wally developed some good friends down there, most of them older than he was. Charlie Nix, a man named Mr. Hartacre, and several others were great fishing cronies. Peggy claimed that Mr. Hartacre, a man in his 70s or 80s would come by every other day or so and ask if Walter could come out and play. If Wally had nothing to do, which he usually didn't, they would push the wooden boat that Wally and Mr Nix owned together out into the Gulf of Mexico and fish all day. My father absolutely loved it, and he never got over his desire for gulf fishing.

Back to Buckeye Country

After the war, in the spring of 1946, my folks moved back to 2417 Abington Road in Columbus, Ohio, actually in Arlington. This was a slightly different time in my father's life. He seemed to be more serious about making his mark and being noted as one of the better achievers in his industry. He also seemed to have more of a desire for the nice things in life— nice cars, nice vacations, golfing.

My actual memories of my father began during this period. Very good at what he did, he became respected as one of the best, not only his company, but in his industry. He attended markets in New York City twice a year. How well I remember them. I used to hate to see him go, believing I could not possibly stand to be two weeks without my dad. I can remember when Mother and Beth and I would drive him down to the old Union Station in downtown Columbus and put him on the train. My tears would flow uncontrollably. But two weeks later when we would drive down to pick him up again, it was just like the Promised Day had come. My good buddy had come home.

A Funny Thing Happened . . .

Years later he told me some of the funny incidents that occurred while he was in New York. One time Wally and three or four other salesmen had invited one of the female buyers up to their room. The salesmen were usually in pretty good with these gals and spent most of their time entertaining them. While the buyers were not supposed to be allowed in the salesmen's rooms, these fellows wanted to give a little dinner for this gal and show her some of the new product lines they had coming out. When they were in the room, one of the fellows was showing this lady buyer a Judo hold that someone had shown him. He was going to try to gently flip her. They were, of course, all tight as ticks, but he got a little too enthusiastic and threw her across the room, breaking her leg. Luckily she was numb enough from liquor that it didn't pain her too much. The only problem they had was in figuring out how to get her out of the hotel and explaining the story without her company's knowing she was in their room. Finally they hit on an idea. Wally got under one of her arms and another fellow got under the other arm. They got on the elevator and walked down to the lobby and started through the lobby acting half drunk, which they were. When they got outside and onto the ice they merely stepped aside and let her go. In one second she was down on the ice, screaming that she had broken her leg. She sued the hotel for damages. What a bunch of bandits!

Wally always had great taxicab driver stories. I don't think there was ever a five-year period in his life when he didn't get in a fist fight with somebody. Taxicab drivers always seemed to be good targets. The New York cab drivers were known to be obnoxious, prone to needling others. If they said something that rankled Wally, he was certainly not averse to telling them what he thought, which would usually end up in an argument. Once he was riding in a cab and was arguing about something. The cab driver slammed on his brakes, and they both got out of the car and went at it. Wally hit the cab driver and broke his jaw, but in the process Wally broke his own thumb. They were standing in front of a hospital so they both just checked into the same hospital. Is this nuts, or what?

Wally's first trip to New York had been highlighted by a cab driver, which may have been the basis for his penchant for arguing with cabbies. On that first trip, he got off the train at the station late at night and had no idea where the hotel was. He was probably only in his late twenties or early thirties. He flagged down a cab and told the fellow he was new in New York and had no idea where his hotel was. Would the fellow please drive him to it. The cab driver seemed to be very accommodating and said he would be glad to help. The night was pitch black. Wally got into the cab, and the driver drove him for about 45 minutes until they finally got to the hotel. My father thanked him very much, gave him a big fee and went into the hotel, glad for a good night's sleep. The next morning when he got up and left the hotel he walked out through the lobby door onto the street; there, right across the street, was the railway station he had just left the night before.

One time Wally was coming into a town on a bus. He had a bout of gastrointestinal distress that day, and he absolutely had to get to the bathroom. Getting off the bus at a run, he rushed to the men's room; it was filled. There would be a wait of several minutes to get a stall, and he simply could not wait. As he ran down the street he saw a hotel, and he headed for it. Rushing through the lobby, he ran straight into the restroom. He got in a stall and closed the door, thankful he had gotten there just in the nick of time. As he was sitting on the commode he heard a woman's high-heeled shoes come clomping over the tiled floor in the bathroom. It then dawned on him that he had gone into the wrong bathroom. The only thing he could do was stand up on the seat of the toilet and bend over so that she would see neither his head nor his shoes. Bad luck being what it is, this gal chose the stall right beside him. He had to crouch in that excruciating position while she came in, lifted her dress, took down her girdle, did her business, then hitched everything back up and left. Wally crept out as cautiously as he could and thanked his lucky stars that nobody had noticed.

PLATE 36. AT HOME ON EAST COOKE ROAD, COLUMBUS, OHIO. The house was a Christmas present for Peg from Wally in 1938; the family lived here in 1943 when Tom II—shown above at age six months with his dad, Walter—was born. In the backyard, right, Wally has a moment with his dad, Tom I.

PLATE 37. INDIAN ROCKS BEACH, FLORIDA. This was the family home from late 1943 to early 1946. It was paradise for the young Chown family.

Right: Tom II and Wally I show off a kingfish.

PLATE 38. BOYHOOD HOME OF TOM II.

Top: The family home in Upper Arlington in Columbus, Ohio (2417 Abington Road), 1946-1959.

Above, right, Tom II with Grandma Sophia in 1949; *left*, Tom II at age 13, 1956.

PLATE 39. WALTER I AND TOM II.

Below: Walter C. Chown I, age 50, 1953. *Right*: Father and son, Walter I and Tom II pose with their catch at Boca Grande, Florida—Tarpon trip. 1958.

ANOTHER BEGINNING: TOM AND BARBARA

PLATE 40. ANOTHER BEGINNING: TOM AND BARBARA.

Barbara Ann (Bain) Chown and Thomas A. Chown II at the time of their wedding, November 28, 1963; both age 20. They recently celebrated their 40th wedding anniversary. Barbara looks about the same as she did 40 years ago . . . Tom doesn't.

PLATE 41.
INTRODUCING TWO
NEW CHOWNS.

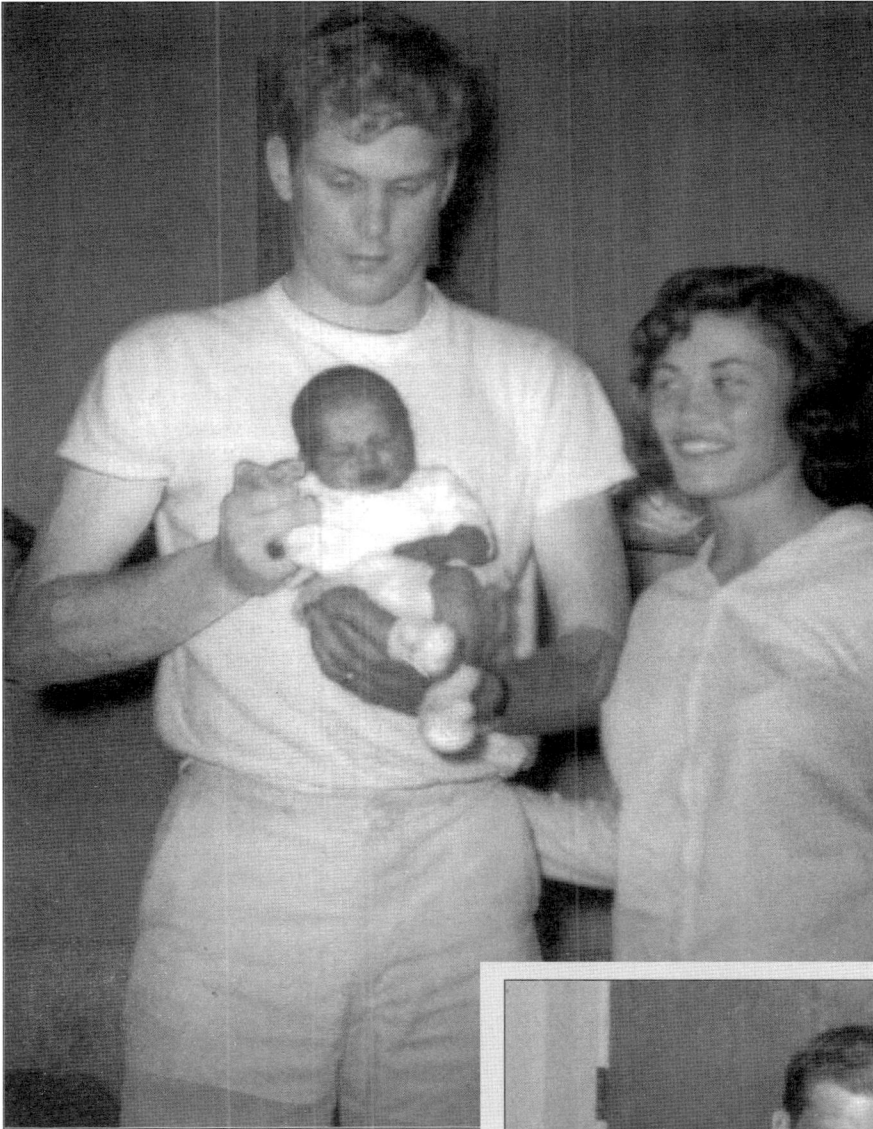

Left: Tom and Barbara
with newborn Lisa Ann
Chown, summer 1964.
Below: Tom with Lisa
and Wally II, 1968.

FAMILY PORTRAIT

PLATE 42. FAMILY PORTRAIT. The Thomas A. Chown II family in 1968. Tom and Barbara, both 25, with their children, Lisa, age four, and Wally, age one year.

PLATE 43. GRANDPARENTS AND PROGENY.

Top: Grandparents in Florida, 1965; left, Peg and Wally Chown; right: Sophia and Joe Butt.

Bottom left: Walter C. Chown II being inspected by Walter C. Chown I, summer 1967.

Bottom right:, one of the last photos of Wally I, here with Wally II and Tom II, September 1969 and Lisa in the background. Wally I died December 6, 1969, about three months after this picture was taken.

NEXT GENERATION

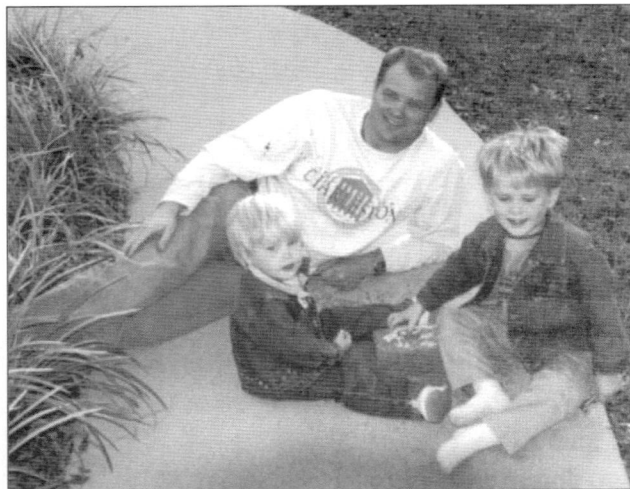

PLATE 44. NEXT GENERATION.

Top, left: Lisa Ann Chown in her high school graduation picture, June 1982, and *right*, Walter C. Chown II in his senior picture, fall 1984.

Bottom left: Lisa Chown Dempsey, her husband, Scott, and their children, Kate, Megan and Michael.

Bottom right: Wally II with his children, Mary Mac and "TAC," Thomas Albert Chown III.

PLATE 45. THE FAMILY'S YOUNGEST.

Top left: The cousins put their heads together; *Top right*, pals Holly and Mr. Higgins.

Directly above: Grandpa Tom and Grandma Barbara on their 40th wedding anniversary, November 28, 2003; the children, left to right: Megan, TAC, Mary Mac, Kate and Michael.

Bottom left: Lisa, Tom II, Barbara and Wally II. *Bottom right*: Mr. Higgins reviews the book.

PLATE 46. CRUISING INTO THE FUTURE TOGETHER: Barbara and Thomas Albert Chown II.

14

Father and Son

THE SCHEDULE I MOST REMEMBER IN MY GROWING UP YEARS IS THE ONE THAT TOOK MY FATHER away on Sunday night and brought him back again Friday afternoon. He worked very hard, and I saw him only on weekends. Even at that I am sure I got more out of my father in one or two days a week than most boys got out of their fathers in seven days.

One time he got into town on a Friday afternoon and was met at the railway station by Lew Colby. Lew came up as though he just happened to be passing by and said "Hi, Walter, how are you doing?"

Wally said, "Fine. Are you down here for any particular reason, Lew?"

"Yes, Walter, now don't get alarmed," Lew replied. "Tommy will be all right, there is nothing seriously wrong with him."

Well my father always believed in getting right to the point and asked Lew what had happened. Again, Lew said, "Now, Walter, I think you should sit down. He is in the hospital but he will be okay. They don't think it's anything really dangerous or serious."

Finally, after he had my father sure that I had not only died but had been in heaven for three days, Lew broke the story. I had accidentally been hit on the head with a baseball bat by Lew's son, Steve, and had six or seven stitches over my left eye. That was no big thing, but my father for years, laughed about how Lew had him absolutely terrified before he would tell him what happened.

On the weekends my father would sometimes load up the car with the kids who lived around our house and drive us down to the swimming pool. Usually my mother did this, but I guess because he was home, this was her chance to have a little time to herself. Dad was sitting on a bench down at the old Devon Road pool in Arlington, and Red Bernard, the father of one of my friends, Rich, was sitting next to him. They had not really met before or, at least, didn't know each other very well. Red asked what my father did for a living, and Dad said he sold girdles.

Red said, "No kidding? Really?" And then he started laughing. He then said, "You don't really sell girdles?" and started laughing again harder. He calmed down and a little while later, after thinking it over, asked my father again if he was serious, then started laughing again, and finally got into a convulsive hysterical laughter over the fact that my father sold girdles. This also tickled my father as he related this story years later, but as far as my dad was concerned, after that he never sold bras and girdles, he sold pot holders and seat covers.

Dad liked his boss, Max Kops, who, on his twenty-first birthday, had been given about a million dollars. He was a very wealthy New York Jew. He was such a gentleman and such a wonderful person that my father, although they came from very diverse backgrounds, felt closely akin to him. They used to have great fun telling stories that were outright fictitious to the buyers while entertaining them. Once Dad and Max sat at dinner and told one particularly gullible buyer about a new girdle they were coming out with made from a new material. It was a breakdown of ostrich feathers that gave the material a very light feel to it. I guess they expanded on that story for an hour or so, and the gal never did catch on that they were pulling her leg.

Dad really loved selling. It was not just as a way to make money; it was also an outlet for his tremendously vivid imagination. He liked to take a product that nobody had been able to sell and make it so appealing that the buyer would almost beg him to sell it to her.

One of Dad's great friends from his corset-selling career was Charlie Joyce. They never worked for the same company, but they had met when they were relatively young and became close friends for the rest of their lives. They both liked to hunt, and together they went on a pheasant hunting trip to South Dakota on two separate occasions. Charlie used to have pretty wild snake dreams. My dad claimed that in the middle of the night Charlie would dream he was thrown into a pit of snakes and start yelling and screaming. He had this dream on three or four different occasions. One time he jumped out of bed and knocked the lamp into the wall, smashing it all over the room. On another occasion he threw his hand out in an effort to get away from the snakes and broke his thumb on the side of the bed. My dad thought that was quite funny.

Most of the men with whom he became good friends were like himself—lusty livers, great drinkers, great partyers, but basically good and clean men. Holly Bell was one of my father's real favorites. He used to tell the story of taking Holly home from a New Year's Eve party three times in one night. Evidently Holly was feeling no pain, and my father took him home and put him to bed. Ten minutes after he got back to the party, he looked across the room and there to his surprise, stood Holly. Dad went over, talked to Holly for a while, got him back into the car, took him home, and put him in bed again. My father came back to the party and, shortly thereafter, in walked Holly. They had some great times together and loved all the fun and activity they could muster up. They used to have a great time trying to see who could out-lie the other or who could outwit the other.

I remember my father from my boyhood days as being very big, very funny, with dark hair, and very tough. It always amazed me when we would be working outside in the cold that I would be absolutely shivering and it never seemed to bother him in the slightest. Also when he would get hurt, if he cut his hand, he never let on that it hurt at all, and it was a rare occasion that he would even bother to put a Band-Aid on it. To me he was a Paul Bunyan if there ever was one. He seemed unusually strong. He regularly tore apples in half. Once I saw him bend a fifty-cent piece with his fingers.

We had some great times together turtle hunting up at Sapps Landing in Mecosta, Michigan. Dad had heard about this place from Dr. Roy Secrest, who lived behind us. On two different occasions my dad and I went up to this lake. Dad actually wanted to fish, but I had gotten the turtle bug, and my wishes won out. For two or three days he did nothing but row me through the lily pads, getting very stiff and quite sunburned. At nights we would go out and drive around the country roads looking for deer. I remember the restaurant we ate in, a lodge up in the hillside, where a waitress would recognize us each night and say, "Well, boys, what do you want this evening?" It was quite a thrill for me to be recognized as "boys" with my father. I was always extremely proud to be his son and to be seen with him.

I remember one time when we were out on one of the lagoons on the lake that I got so excited trying to catch a Blanding turtle that I dove out of the boat after the turtle. Dad got extremely upset, thinking I was going to drown. He would always be nervous when I sat up in the front of the boat, fearing I might fall over and get caught in the motor. All in all on the turtle hunting trip, we got about 80 turtles. I had talked my dad into helping me build a little concrete pond in our back yard with a fenced-in area around it. When we got home, I put the turtles in there, and it was quite a menagerie. As a matter of fact, I was written up by a local columnist, Johnny Jones, in the Columbus Dispatch. I would sell the turtles to neighborhood kids for a dollar apiece. Then when their mothers would refuse to let them in their house, the kids would bring them back to my pond. There was no refund, and I'm sure I sold many a turtle three or four times.

Some of the things I did to the back yard that my father put up with were amazing. Once at Fort Scott Summer Camp I learned to high jump. I thought that was great fun and asked him on a Sunday evening if I could put a little high jump pit in the back yard. Partly because he had been a high jumper back in his high school days, he thought this would be fine for me. He figured I intended to put up a couple of standards with nails in them that I could hang a bamboo pole across. When he came home on Friday, I had dug a pit right in the middle of the back yard about a foot deep, about eight feet long and four feet wide . . . and had filled it with sawdust. He was irate when he pulled in and saw it, but after he calmed down he decided that as long as it was there he might as well show me how to high jump. When he was in college he tried to high jump in street shoes once and had broken his arm. This time when he tried to show me how to high jump in his street shoes, he didn't break his arm, only his watch. The time in high school when he broke his arm, he was at the doctor's office having it checked. The doctor noticed there was something strange about the way the bone was healing. He had my father look out the window at a particular bird, and when he looked out the window, the doctor broke his arm again right over his leg. It had been setting incorrectly and he had to reset it.

The Apple Doesn't Fall Far . . .

Some of the incidents when I was a boy on Abington Road involving my father were really funny, but I'm not particularly proud of them. Steve Colby and I were horsing around in the back yard once and broke the frame on a nice new lawn chair my dad had just purchased. It was a weekend, and Dad had just come home from playing golf. He was in the kitchen fixing himself a drink and was going to come out and relax in the back yard. Steve and I reconstructed the chair just enough so that it would stand, but a good breeze would have knocked it over. We then hid in the garage and watched. My father came through the back door with his drink in his hand and an obvious look of pleasure as he was about to sit down and relax. He straddled over the chair and lowered his body into it, whereupon the whole thing collapsed and his drink went all over him. He got up cussing at the chair, declaring they didn't make things the way they used to.

Another time, Steve and I decided to find out if a cherry bomb would explode under water. We got out my father's brand new minnow bucket, filled it with water and dropped in the cherry bomb, never dreaming it would just shred the sides of the minnow bucket as though it had been hit with a shotgun. Not knowing what to do, we put the minnow bucket under the work bench. That following spring when my father came out to get it, he remarked about the lousy material the bucket was made of, rusting through so quick like that.

There was another time when either Steve or I kicked a football way up into the top of one of the trees in our front yard. We threw balls at it, we threw baseball gloves at it, we threw bats at it, we threw everything we could think of to get that football down from where it was lodged in the tree. No luck. My father figured the best thing to do was blow the branch off right below it, thereby freeing the ball. He fired the shotgun at the branch okay, but instead of just clipping it off, he blew the whole branch, ball—everything— right out of the tree, and when it came down, the football just collapsed because all of the air had leaked out of it. You could hear the shotgun pellets in it if you shook it.

Another time Dad was going to hit my football on the grass with a slingshot to teach me how to operate a slingshot. He hauled off and shot at the ball and, sure enough, he hit it, but the rock he used careened off the ball and went right through Mrs. Kohler's window. A couple of weeks later he was going to show me how to throw a curve ball with a tennis ball. He succeeded in curving it enough to send it through the exact same window the slingshot rock had gone through. Again, we were off to the hardware store to buy replacement glass.

Another time my dad's color-blindness got him into trouble. We had a green parakeet named Pancho that flew freely around the house. One time when a neighbor opened the back door, Pancho flew out. We mustered every available kid and willing adult to help us chase Pancho down. When we spotted him sitting on a high tree branch, it seemed logical to us to throw balls at him, trying to get him down. Lower and lower Pancho flew, but he was tiring fast. Finally he flew into a big juniper bush on the corner of Abington and Asbury roads. Our entire crew surrounded the bush. This time Pancho was low enough that we could prod him to get him out, and we used nearly everything at hand—golf clubs, rakes, tennis rackets. Suddenly Pancho broke, flying right over Dad, who had a tennis racket in his hand. Reflexively Dad "served" ol' Pancho, smacking him pretty hard. However, the bird seemed okay, and we placed him back in his cage. The next day when I returned home from school, I went to the cage to check on Pancho. In the cage was a very pretty, but very blue, parakeet.

"Where's Pancho?" I asked Dad.

"Right there in his cage," Dad replied.

"That isn't Pancho," I said.

Dad finally owned up. He had found Pancho dead as a doornail in his cage that morning. In a panic, Dad rushed out and bought what he thought was a dead ringer for Pancho, but Dad was color blind. This little episode was forever known as the failed bird caper!

We always had great times on vacations. He was a real believer in taking family vacations even when we probably couldn't afford to do so. We went to Florida almost every other year the whole time I was growing up. In between we had a vacation through New England, my mother having been raised in Worcester, Massachusetts. That was a nice trip, and I remember my father's great joy when he discovered that Earl Pattenaud, a fireman and one of my mother's early boyfriends, was now totally bald. We had an extensive journey on that trip, covering most of the New England states.

Another time we went to Williamsburg and then down to the islands off North Carolina—places such as Kitty Hawk and Nag's Head. I remember seeing a movie on the Declaration of Independence in Williamsburg. At the end of the movie the colonists were all standing around waiting to see if their officials would vote for independence. When they did, the window of the building they were in flew open, everybody looked out and the American Flag went up on the staff. The movie was then over and the lights came on. I remember my father taking his handkerchief out of his pocket to wipe the tears away from his eyes. He had really become emotionally involved in the United States Flag, a fact that, at the time, I could not understand. Now, I have a similar feeling every time I see the U.S. flag go up.

We went to Milwaukee to visit my grandparents, then went up into northern Wisconsin with Grandpa Butt and fished for a while, leaving my mother with her mother in Milwaukee. A year or two later we went up to Wisconsin and Michigan and visited the Sioux Locks. On Lake Superior once, my father thought it was funny to sneak around and film my mother going to the bathroom behind a bush. It was a long stretch of beach on the far side of Lake Superior where there are no towns, people or anything else worth mentioning. When we got home, Dad didn't say a word about his secret filming; he just rolled the film. My mother didn't seem to think it was so funny; he had to cut and splice to get the offensive footage out of the home movies.

Dad was a tremendous snorer. On every one of our trips it drove us nuts having to listen to him snore all night. Finally, by agreement, we all put our slippers beside our beds as ammunition. During the night when he would reach a real crescendo, one of us would reach over, grab one slipper and hit him on the back of the head with it from across the room. That would usually slow him down for ten or fifteen minutes until he would reach a peak again, whereupon we would do it again. He was the world champion snorer.

Because Dad and Max Kops were such good friends, Dad agreed to let Max's son, George, live at our house for a while, generally supervising him while he was a freshman at Ohio State University. Being a New York City boy, Max thought it would be good for George to go to a midwestern college. George was a real hell-raiser and a heck of a nice guy, but my father had some problematic episodes with him. I remember one time when George was arrested for drunk driving and had to spend a night in the drunk tank. Dad thought it would be a good example for me to go down with him when he bailed George out of jail. That was quite an experience, going into the Columbus City Jail and bailing out old George, who then had to report for three days of labor. That pretty well convinced him that drunk driving was not the best thing to do. It convinced me of that fact, also.

George flunked out of college once and was going to just out-and-out leave, but my father persuaded the University officials to let him back in. This was an incident that Max never found out about. George dropped out again and joined the U.S. Marines. After about two years in the marines, he got back in school and was a good student getting much better grades and seeming much more serious.

My father had some unusual health problems. I remember his tendency to choke on steaks. I don't know whether he didn't chew properly or what, but on more than one occasion mother, Beth and I had to literally drag him from his chair in the dining room to the bathroom and let him get some water and cough the steak out into the toilet. Once he was absolutely purple before he dislodged the steak from his windpipe. I was sure he was on his way out. Another time he jumped into a cold shower after mowing the lawn on a hot day, and fell in the shower. He collapsed and passed out because, he explained, he had been hit on the head in Chicago years earlier and had gotten a type of concussion. He said they had been walking down a sidewalk and some punks made some comment to my mother. My father started fighting with one of them, and another hit him on the head with a blackjack. He was unconscious for about three days, and all of his life he had a resulting problem with occasionally blacking out. (Another of those bizarre stories!)

I remember worrying very much about him when I was young, concerning religion. I went to school at St. Agatha's Church and was taught to believe that Catholicism was the only way (which, of course, I now know is a load of hooey). My father had been raised as a strict Catholic, had served as an altar boy and had been around priests all his life. As an adult, however, he totally rejected the idea of organized, church-going religion. I was sure that if he died he was going to go straight to hell, even though he was my daddy and I loved him very much. As I grew older, I realized that even though he was not a church-going man he had a strong sense of kindness, honesty (other than the aforementioned mirror-stealing incident) and charity toward others. I think every person who knew Walter Chown benefited in some way from knowing him. He got one or two jobs for Charlie Joyce. As the years went by, Dad became the general crying post for most of the men in his industry. I remember on many occasions his work partners or just friends coming to the house to have him help solve their problems. He didn't need to be a church-goer to be a really good man.

When I was in high school, the relationship he and I had was special. There came a time when he began coaching me on how to be a man and thinking of me less as a little boy. In sports I always tried to equal the records he had set and never really did. He was a tremendous natural athlete, had been a good football and baseball player and was good in golf with little or no practice. When he watched me play sports, such as basketball, he would always encourage me to shoot more. He couldn't understand why I wasn't more aggressive. I remember after the Delaware basketball game once I had gotten in a fight with one of the Delaware town "hoods." The fellow had hit me in the jaw, but then I knocked him down a flight of stairs. When I reported this to my parents, my mother was aghast, but I'll never forget the look of satisfaction on my father's face as he was trying to tell me the evils of fist fighting.

End of the Story

It was at this point in the 1970 narrative that I, apparently, ran out of gas. Perhaps I simply got busy with life and trying to raise my own family. For whatever reason, I abruptly stopped, except for a hand-written note at the end of my typed story: "not yet finished, I'll continue someday." So here I am, after a brief 33-year trip to the bathroom, ready to continue the story.

Looking back at that time, 1970, I realize how much shock and grief over his death I still felt, one year after his death, when I was a mere 27 years of age. My view of him was, of course, that of a boy, or a very young man. I clearly had a case of hero worship involving him. I still do . . . and most likely always will.

Yet in the 33 years since I wrote the original narrative about my dad, all the above, I have grown up . . . and old. I had never known my father when he was 27. He was 40 when I was born. In five years, I myself will be 66, the same age he was when he died. (It is not lost on me that, in addition to my father's being 66 at his death, his father, Tom, was 67 when he died. That's why I'm writing fast!) I now have a different perspective on my father. As I age I can empathize with his struggles and joys. I can even understand the lives of his father, Tom, and grandfather Bill better as I get further down the path myself. And so I continue the story of Walter C. Chown I, from my 61-year-old memory and perspective, from about 1959 to his death on December 6, 1969.

Let me begin by making what I think is a significant observation, one that illuminates the perspective of people of my father's particular life span. My father was born in 1903, which happens to be the year of the Wright brothers "First Flight." And he died in 1969, the year Neil Armstrong took that "giant leap for mankind" on the moon. Wow! The early years were almost primitive when viewed against the backdrop of the progressive 1950s and 1960s. Think of a lifetime in which lynchings and "colored bathrooms" were somewhat normal but also included the subsequent, far-reaching civil rights legislation. My life has included change too, of course. (For example, there was no TV in my birth year of 1943.) I think we would be hard pressed to find any age, however, with a larger "sea change" of culture and lifestyle than the life span of my parents. (I guess the biggest change in my life is the computer and resulting high tech world, plus an almost complete collapse of our family-oriented moral structure.)

Probably the single most defining event in my father's life as he approached the 1960s was a massive heart attack he had in the fall of 1960. I was just starting my senior year at Upper Arlington High School. I remember my mother's getting the call that Dad had had the attack in Pittsburgh, Pennsylvania, on a routine sales trip. It was in October during a world series game. She and I immediately packed suitcases and jumped in the car for Pittsburgh. It was a scary time, but he pulled through to face six months to a year of recovery efforts, the first few months in a wheelchair. I believe that near death experience had a marked effect on him, for he seemed to understand the reality of his own mortality from then on.

He and my mother had built a beautiful new home at 3200 Halesworth Road, at the corner of Trentwood Road, just north of the "new" high school in Upper Arlington. He would have been about 55 years old when they moved into it in 1958. Both he and my mother had worked very hard, he with his sales career and she with the Peggy Chown Shop, a women's foundation garment specialty store they opened in Lane Avenue Shopping Center in 1950.

I had loved the Abington Road house, but it was a bit small, and they were following the "upwardly mobile" American Dream of hard work rewarded. I am certain my father never forgot the relative hard times and poverty of his youth, and the raw existence of his father in Colorado. I am also sure it meant a lot to him for his family, friends, and the whole world to know he and my mother were "successful." The Halesworth home was built by George Stegmiller, the most prestigious builder at the time in Columbus, who had built one or two of

Jack Nicklaus' first homes in Arlington. I was in cub scouts with the builder's son, John. He and I went to high school and college together, and we are still friends.

When we moved into the new house I was 15. I had become quite smitten with "shooting pool" with my Abington Road neighbor and great boyhood friend, Steve Colby. After seeing an ad in the paper for an old pool table, I bought it with my own money for $150, which I had saved from having two paper routes. (I had delivered the morning Columbus Citizen Journal and the afternoon Columbus Dispatch for a couple of years.) I refinished the old Brunswick (made in about 1900 and found in a defunct Belle Fontaine, Ohio, pool hall) and reassembled it in our new basement. We all, especially my dad and I, really enjoyed it. He relived his "ill-spent youth" on it with me and my friends. That pool table was a catalyst for many hours of hilarity and tall tales for my friends Bob McKnight, Ken Clark, Mike Mandt and others, including my father. I'm sure I realized what a character Walter Chown was prior to my buying the pool table. But interacting with him on a more man-to-man basis, and seeing him captivate my best friends with his gloriously oversized personality and sense of humor was just terrific. He was really at the top of his game in 1958 and 1959. He was the top salesman in his industry nationally. He was proud of himself, my mother, and, I believe, me. Things were just great . . . until the heart attack in October 1960.

Actually, even after the recovery period, things were still great, but different. The doctor had told him to stop smoking or die. He had been a two-and-a-half-pack (of unfiltered Camels) per day man, and a two-fisted straight scotch (Black and White) drinker. In the absence of the cigarettes he started in on candy Life Savers. He went from about 170 lbs to 215 lbs in six months. The doctor said, "Hell, Walter, if you're going to eat yourself to death you might as well smoke yourself to death." And he basically did. From about 1961 on , I think he figured he was on borrowed time anyway, so he might as well live exactly the way he wanted. He went back to smoking, although, I think, he tried filters. If anything, I believe his scotch drinking increased.

He and Mother and good friends Frank and Sybil McClelland took a trip to the Florida Keys in early 1961. It was my father's first "break out" trip after several recoup months and produced an incident which typified his attitude for the rest of his life.

Just prior to the trip he bought a new 1960 black Buick Electra convertible, with red and white interior. Very flashy . . . very un-Walter "Four-Door Sedan" Chown. Very "I'm probably not long for this world so I might as well live it up." Anyway, he and Mom and the McClellands pulled over to take a break just off the road on one of the bridges on US 1, the "Overseas Highway." It was time for one of my father's medicine breaks.

Here's the way he told it:

> I was standing there chatting with Frank while I began rummaging through my shoe box filled with pill bottles. Let's see, do I take two green ones, one red, two whites and a blue pill now? Or is it two red, three blues, one orange and a purple? After getting totally confused, frustrated and irritated by my dilemma, I came up with a solution. I simply threw the whole box off the bridge into Florida Bay! Problem solved!

From then on, to the best of my knowledge, the only heart-related pill he took was the occasional digitalis.

Another really grim occurrence related to his heart problem manifested itself in his teeth. Somewhere in the early 1960s his teeth got wobbly in his gums. The dentist explained that something having to do with his heart (poor circulation?) had caused the roots in his teeth to whither. All his teeth had to come out . . . but without any anesthesia due to his heart condition. They started this painful process by yanking three or four at a sitting, letting them heal for a week or two, then back for another three or four. Finally after several weeks of this torture, Dad could stand no more. He went back in with five or six left and said, "Dammit, this is it . . . pull 'em all and get it over with." The dentist complied. On the way home in the car Dad began to gag from the pain. He pulled off the road, threw open the door, and in jerking awkwardly out and down to throw up . . . he snapped three ribs! Talk about a hard luck story!

What I remember most about my father in those years was what seemed to be an endless stream of events caused by the difficult transition of a middle aged man into old age. An unhealthy-heart-old-age to boot. He still wanted to rip 'n' snort. He still wanted to outsell all competition. He still wanted to play golf, shoot pool, tell jokes and be the life of every party. And to an amazing degree, he did. At his funeral in 1969, an old friend said to me, "When Walter Chown walked in a room, everybody knew it."   Another old friend, actually a long time friendly competitor of his, Joe Casey, said to me, "Tom, the only thing I can say to sum up your dad is . . . there was one hellava man! He outdid us all over the thirty plus years I was privileged to know him in selling, befriending, laughing, story telling, golfing, drinking and card playing. He was the most honest, competitive and loveable guy I ever knew. There'll never be another like him."

It is interesting to be the son of a "larger than life" man. My memories of him in my extreme youth, under ten or twelve, were of a very tall (six feet, two-and-a-halfinches), dark haired, extremely confident man. He spoke and the world jumped . . . or laughed. Because he was 40 when I was born, my early memories were of him in his mid-forties up to his mid-fifties . . . then the heart attack when he was about 57. Not only was he greatly changed, so were my mother and I, as well. As anyone knows who has lived with a family member with a serious health problem, you are constantly waiting for the "other shoe to drop." My mother would tell me she subconsciously listened for his breathing all night. If he skipped a breath or abruptly stopped snoring, she'd panic until he breathed again. I know I lived in great fear of losing him, my all-time best friend . . . which, of course, eventually happened in 1969.

But! As morose as all of this is beginning to sound, the situation also had a very positive effect. Knowing that Walter Chown was most likely living on borrowed time made us all, I believe, really relish the many good, great and hilarious times we had through the 1960s.

Wally and Peg went to Hawaii in 1962. I was a freshman at Miami University in Oxford, Ohio. They had just sold the Peggy Chown Shop and were celebrating Wally's semi-recovery with proceeds from that sale. Plus, he was back on his feet and doing, as always, very well in his sales career. The photos, slides and, especially, the super-eight movies of that "trip of a lifetime" to Hawaii show a couple very much in love. They had financial success and a son off to college. Beth, who was five years older than I, had failed out of Ohio State, was in the first of three failed marriages and well on the path to being a constant source of misery and heart break to her adoptive parents. From the day they adopted Beth as an infant in 1938, our parents gave her all the love and help they knew how, and watched her make every bad and ruinous decision it was possible to make. She was the only "fly in the ointment" in what was an otherwise "Ozzie and Harriet" type family in those years.

In addition to Hawaii, my father again went against all previous tendencies by trading a Buick sedan for a brand new 1962 gold Buick Riviera, a low-slung, two-seat sports type vehicle—hardly what he should have been driving to cover the Midwest selling bras and girdles. But as a freshman and sophomore at Miami University, I loved it. For a brief time, he and Mother had the Electra convertible and the Riviera, which I absolutely couldn't believe. While still in high school, I had bought an old 1953 blue Chevy BelAir as my own car. It would take me anywhere I wanted to go but, unfortunately, would never bring me back. (My friend Bob McKnight will attest to this.) But to have a stable of these sexy Buicks for dates was really a "coup" for me. In retrospect, I don't know if my dad's fling with hot cars was for himself (to go out "in style") or for me. Maybe he thought I'd remember him more lovingly. But in any event, they didn't last long. By about 1964, he must have figured he'd had his automotive pizzazz, or he figured he wasn't going to die right away after all, or he figured these cars (especially the Riviera) were just too cramped for a six-foot, two-inch stiff old geezer to be getting in and out of. (Man, can I relate to that now!) So he traded them off and went back to four-door brown or beige Buick sedans. Having jazzy cars was great while it lasted.

When I myself finally realized he wasn't going to drop dead immediately, I started treating him a little differently. By 1962 and '63 I had become quite disenchanted with college. Actually, I was at loose ends with life in general. A college friend, George Bailey, and I agreed to drop out of school, meet in New Orleans, and take a tramp steamer around the world. Sounds perfectly plausible doesn't it? Well, somehow, it did sound reasonable to me in the winter of my discontent, 1962-63.

Since this is my father's story, not mine, I will keep this brief. I can only imagine what he and my mother must have thought about my departure from sanity at that time. In a nutshell, I went back to Oxford after Christmas break for trimester exams, for which I had not studied. I came within a hundredth of a point of flunking out.

I called my father and said, "Pick me up, I'm done. College life isn't for me. I'm going to hitch-hike to Florida, then New Orleans and then, around the world. . . . I quit."

"Fine," he said. "I'll pick you up Saturday morning."

Well, that didn't go so bad, I thought. No big lecture, no argument. He must understand my position. After all, he did his own following the wheat harvest in Kansas and lumber jacking in Montana when he was young. And to think, I was worried he might be upset. What a guy!

Well, Saturday came and up he pulled in front of my rooming house on North Bishop Street in Oxford. As he moved over to the passenger side, I came enthusiastically down with my suitcases and large dirty laundry bag, threw them in the trunk and popped in the driver's side. "Morning, Daddy [I always called him Daddy], how you doin?"

"You, sir, are a bum," he declared. "You truly are a lazy, good-for-nothing, going-nowhere no-good bum. Let me give you a brief family history lesson. Your grandfather, for whom you are so unworthily named, worked in coal mines and on absolutely barren Colorado plains trying to eke out a living. He did all he could for me but died broke from the Depression and the Dust Storms. I dropped out of Marquette out of necessity. I worked myself into a nervous breakdown but finally got into a sales job. With no education or profession, I've had no other choice but to start every January first at square one and work my butt off to feed you and your sister. Same with your mother. She has run the shop the last ten years just to save enough for your college education."

He barely took a breath before continuing: "There has never been a college graduate in our family, and we both were setting all our hopes and efforts on you! We worked to make it easy for you by paying for it totally. We didn't want you to have to work or get loans . . . just study and become something . . . be somebody . . . get a profession. But, no, you want to jump a boat and see the world. Well, fine. Your mother didn't come because she's home crying and didn't want to say anything unkind to you. Well, I don't know if this is considered unkind, Tom, but I'll tell you once again, you are a bum! A God-damned bum. And as far as I can see, you always will be!! Now start the car and let's go home, quitter."

Apparently I had slightly underestimated my father's level of pique about my plans. It was a long, very quiet ride home, and at the end of it I was greeted by my equally heart-broken, if less vociferous, mother. I mention this story only to point out at least one juncture at which my relationship with my dad began to change. This was probably the first time I was not securely ensconced in the Golden Boy chair in my parents' home. Mercifully, this event had no lasting effect on our love and respect for each other. I did hitch-hike to and all around Florida in early 1963. I stood at the I-10 exit just north of Tallahassee in a snowstorm, with only my cotton madras shirt and light parka, staring at the sign: New Orleans . . . thataway. Atlanta and home . . . t'otherway. I thought about George Bailey and the tramp steamer in New Orleans, and I thought about home. I thought and thought . . . for what must have been an hour or more . . . freezing my butt off.

Finally I thought, My dad's right, I am a bum! Screw it. I'm going home, enroll in Ohio State, and finish this job! (I never heard from George Bailey again. I have no idea if he got to New Orleans, or like me, chickened out. I hope he's having a good life!) I hitch-hiked back to Charleston, South Carolina and ran out of money. My hitch rides were more of an education than I had ever had, but that's for a different narrative. I called my dad and said I was almost broke, cold and pretty miserable. He was right, I was a bum, but I had seen the light. If he would give me one more chance, I'd make good. And by the way, could he pick me up at the Greyhound station downtown Columbus the next night at 2:38 a.m.?

If you've never taken a 500-mile bus ride . . . don't. That bus stopped at every little hamlet and picked up every wino whacko along the way. And it's just bumpy and uncomfortable enough to keep you from sleeping. And with no money, no eatee! The bus pulled in, I got off, and there was that dear, dear man. He hugged me and said, "Welcome home, Big Boy. Could you use a steak?" Phew! As I said, what a guy!

15

Man-to-Man

I AM STILL CLOSING IN ON THE CHANGING RELATIONSHIP I HAD WITH MY DAD. I HAVE LEFT OUT the real reason I came back. Although my sudden epiphany as to my father's correct assessment of my true worth was a factor, I had unknowingly developed another strong reason to go home. Her name was Barbara Ann Bain. Our meeting, dating and marriage is a story unto itself, but this is my dad's story, not mine. I mention Barbara because after we married in November, 1963, I could relate to my father as a married man. And after Lisa and Wally (Walter C. Chown II) were born, I related to Dad as a family man. And after I finally graduated from Ohio State in 1965 and began my sales career with John Hancock, we had even more in common. I won a few sales achievement awards and got my name in the paper a couple of times, which seemed to make him proud.

One event that made me take notice of him involved the purchase of our first home, the little red house at 2266 Woodstock Road. Barbara's dad, Emmett Bain, found the ad for it in the paper. We went to see it and liked it, although it was tiny. The firm price was $17,500. We took my mother and father through it, and they agreed it was a good starter home. Since I was a college graduate and had just started with John Hancock (this was 1965), our Realtor filled out the sales contract and loan papers and assured us we would have no trouble getting approved. He calculated our monthly payments over thirty years, and we believed we could handle it. All the while my dad just sat quietly in the corner.

Finally the Realtor said, "Well, if this all looks good, sign here."

Then my father spoke. "That won't be necessary," he said, and he made out a check for $17,500 to the owner.

Well, we just about fainted. He told us we could pay him on an agreed-upon schedule . . . interest free. Today, $17,500 is about what you pay for a middle-of-the road used car, but back then, especially to Barb and me, it was Fort Knox. I was flabbergasted, not only by his ability to write a check for that amount, but also that he would.

In retrospect, I believe he knew his time with us on this earth was limited, and he wanted to do all he could to help us. After we moved in, it was not unusual for us to semi-sleep in on a Saturday or Sunday morning and wake to the sound of his trimming bushes or fixing something in the backyard. I think he just liked being around our little family and being a helpful part of it. Same with my mother. And the house purchase was only one of many times they helped us financially. I'm not proud that we needed a few bucks now and then, but we were extremely grateful to get it. They took us on several vacations and paid for it—Florida, Lake Erie and French Lick, Indiana, come to mind. And as Barbara's parents also kindly did, they babysat . . . a lot!

Part of the fun my dad and I had involved golf. We played as a foursome—Dad, Mom, Barb and I—fairly often. That was not always easy because of my mother and Barbara. Mom (Barb's mother-in-law) was a long time very good golfer. Barbara (daughter-in-law) was a novice hacker. At times, they were a bit like "water and oil" on the golf course. But Dad and I were on the same level. He had been a pretty good player in his forties and fifties, especially so in that he didn't have time to play much. My parents had joined Brookside Country Club, north of Arlington, for a few years in the late 1940s and early 1950s, and we still have a trophy he won in 1949 as flight winner in a tournament. He shot a couple of rounds in the high 70s and was mostly in the low- to mid-80s back then.

After that they got busier with his job, the new house, the Peggy Chown Shop and raising kids, and they dropped the membership. Then, of course, there was the heart attack. Before I was married, I didn't play golf, other than a few rounds with Steve Colby in my early teens. So when my father and I began enjoying each other's company on the links, we were both about equal. On the Gray Course at Ohio State, both of us were in the mid- to high-80s. On the Scarlet Course we were low- to mid-90s.

We really had fun at it. For those roughly five years from 1964-1969 we played, as I said as couples and also just father and son. As couples, he did his best to break Barb in, so to speak. She was really suffering learning the game—the rules, the skills, the etiquette. When it was apparent she was just about to crack, he'd replace her ball with an exploding one or a lopsided one, just to create humor. He could get away with more as the father-in-law than I could as her husband. We all tried to keep humor in the game, which must have worked because Barb finally fit in, and to this day she greatly enjoys golf.

When we played as singles, I really enjoyed Dad's company. We talked about everything and nothing. Two funny events I remember happened at OSU. Since I generally out-drove him off the tee and I usually drove the cart, it was my custom to go to his ball first, then mine. Sometimes I'd be so exuberant about my "long drive," I'd forget to stop at his first. Once I did this a couple of times in the first nine, to his displeasure. When I did it a third time he said, "Listen, slugger, would it be too much to ask you to stop at my ball?" I knew he was rightfully annoyed, so I whipped around on a dime and headed back to his ball. Not looking directly at him I continued with whatever wisdom I was regaling him with as we got back to his ball. When I turned to him to see what club he'd choose I happened to notice . . . he wasn't in the cart. I had thrown him out when I wheeled the cart around way up the fairway. His language as I went back to retrieve him is not fit for this family chronology.

The other episode wasn't my fault, but it had the potential for disaster. Again, I was driving the cart as we approached a long narrow bridge over a lake at OSU; I don't recall whether it was the Scarlet or Gray course. My father mentioned that the asphalt pathway over the lake looked kind of crumbly. As I hit the bridge and we got about halfway across, the asphalt road started to disintegrate beneath us. I sped up, with whole chunks dropping into the lake as we passed over the bridge. We finally shot off the far end of the bridge, none the worse for wear. Even if we had gone through and into the drink, probably about the worst result would have been a good soaking. The adventure gave us one more thing to enjoy and laugh about together.

More Good Times

It seems the last few years of his life I kept doing things to get his goat. Once I borrowed his 18-foot runabout boat to take my "little brother" fishing on the Scioto River. This story is really too long to do it justice here. The punch line, however, is that the engine conked out way, way up river, and I couldn't restart it. After laboriously getting the car (one of Dad's brown four-door Buicks) and trailer through a farm field and positioned to pull out the boat, I made a small mistake. I hit the wrong gear on the transmission putting it in neutral and backed the trailer and car right into the river! Had to then call a tow truck to retrieve boat, trailer and car all in one effort. The back floor carpet of the car was soaked with river water, which I did my best to dry out before Dad got back in town. He never knew what happened, but he did comment that the car "smelled odd . . . sort of musty . . . almost fishy"—especially when the windows were rolled up.

Another time, an innocent prank I pulled on him had an unexpected ending involving a bullet hole—not a real one but one of those fake decals you put on a window that is supposed to look like a real bullet hole. He was still actively traveling in his work and had recently been in Detroit. This was in about 1968 when lots of racial unrest was breaking into violence in major northern cities. He told us there had been several shootings in downtown Detroit when he was last there, and if not a big concern, it was at least something to be aware of. Well, when he was due to head up to "Motown" again in several weeks, I got a bright idea. Someone had given me one of the aforementioned decals. After Barb and I and the kids had Sunday dinner at Mom and Dad's, we said our goodbyes and left via the garage. He was leaving early Monday morning for Detroit. On the way through the garage I casually stuck the decal on the passenger side window of his car . . . and promptly forgot about it.

The next Saturday morning I stopped by their house early for some reason. In passing I asked, "How was your Detroit trip?" He looked both ways and put his fingers to his lips. "Don't tell your mother, but I got shot at!"

"What?" I exclaimed. "How could that happen? What do you mean?" And then I froze with realization of my culpability.

"Yeah, some son of a bitch shot the far window. I only noticed it on the way home yesterday, so I don't know when it happened, but I wheeled into Daniel's Buick and had Art replace the window before your mother saw it."

Before I could confess he swore me to secrecy so as not to alarm Mom. I did not confess. I took the oath of secrecy. And to this day I don't know if I fooled him . . . or he fooled me. When I asked if he took a real good look at the "bullet hole" he said no. It unnerved him so much he just parked it at the service bay, pointed at it to Art, his long time favorite mechanic, and told him to slap in a new window. Maybe Art fooled us both.

Another Detroit happening that occurred at about the same time as the racial unrest involved a young black parking attendant. Dad gave the fellow his ticket and the guy went to get the car. After 15 minutes or so, Dad walked back through the lot and found the young man sitting in Dad's car with the radio blaring. After exchanging some verbal "pleasantries," he finally set his briefcase down and took a swing at the attendant. He missed and the guy knocked Dad over his own briefcase; he had the black eye to prove it. It had nothing to do with race. He just thought the young guy needed a kick in the butt . . . which he failed to administer! Apparently this young whipper-snapper failed to realize he was dealing with the 1924 heavyweight boxing champ at Marquette Academy.

As the sixties waned, Peg and Wally seemed to really enjoy life. I know he was wearing down because he told me so. There were numerous times when he'd just gotten home after spending another few days or a week on the road, and we would stop by. He'd be slumped in his chair . . . usually with a scotch beside him. He never actually exercised, although he remained active. He ate well only under Mom's guidance . . . I'm sure not well at all on the road. And there was the constant smoking. I remember his pajama tops had little burn holes in them where he had a lit cigarette in his mouth even before removing his PJs. And the heart condition was still there. He said he was worn out, and I'm sure he was. But . . . he kept at everything.

Unusual Double Death

In May of 1968 my mother's mother and step-father died within a day of each other . . . from natural causes. I will mention my mother in a little more detail in awhile, but a bit of back ground is needed now. Even though this is my dad's part of the story, as we have seen with past Chowns, the wives have great influence on their men's lives.

Margaret Emily Mathews (one "T" she always stressed) was born in Manchester, England, July 11, 1906, to one Charles Mathews and his 16-year-old wife—or girlfriend?— Sophia Balkes. She had been born in Germany but later sent to England to learn to be a seamstress. She met Charles Mathews, an Englishman, and had her only child, my mother. Mathews went to America, specifically Worcester, Massachusetts, and then sent for his wife and daughter. My mother, Margaret (Peggy), said she was little more than an almost infant and had no memory of the trip. Her father was, in her account, normal, until he deserted them when she was a pre-teen, probably ten or younger. Peg never seemed at all effected by him or his absence, but was always very close to her mother. Eventually, probably in the early 1930s, Sophia married a guy named Joe Butt (your eyes are not playing tricks on you . . . and that's another story). They moved to Milwaukee to be closer to their married daughter Margaret, who had been "Peg" Chown since 1926. When Peg and Wally moved with his sales territories to such places as Chicago, Peoria and Indianapolis, Joe and Sophia stayed put in Milwaukee.

As a little kid, born and raised in Columbus, Ohio, I remember many wonderful visits to Grandma and Grandpa Butt at 4447 South Austin Street, on Milwaukee's south side. Then, in about 1959 or 1960, I believe, they moved to Columbus. They bought a tiny little brick home on Beechwold Street in the north end. I'm relating all this to explain the events in my dad's life that resulted from this move.

Wally had a great relationship with Sophia and Joe. Although Joe was a hen-pecked, mealy-mouthed mumbler, small of stature and with no presence to speak of and Walter was a loud, fun-loving, outgoing, charismatic salesman type, they got along just fine. I remember a couple of occasions when Walter blew up at them for secretly trying to remove tip money from the table in restaurants because they thought he had left too much.

"Jesus Christ, Joe [or Mother], put that tip back on the table where I left it. You haven't paid for a meal or left a tip in ten years, so don't worry about what I leave!"

They'd put the money back and skulk out, and all would be forgiven.

Anyway, they lived in Columbus, were over at my parents' house frequently, and we saw them a lot. Sophia and Barb, literally, got off on the wrong foot when they first met. Sophia kept staring at Barb's feet and finally asked if they were purple from stamping on all those grapes (Barbara is half Italian). The joke didn't go over extremely well, but soon all was forgiven. Grandma Butt became "Gay Gay" Butt to Lisa as an infant; young Wally never really knew her. It is hard to associate the name "Gay Gay" with a German lady with all the cuddlyness of Adolf Eichmann! But she was great and I loved her, as I imagine my father sort of did, and I know my mom did.

And then they died. Barbara and I got a call late one evening from my dad, from Grandma and Grandpa's house, that Joe had died. They had been sitting peacefully in side-by-side chairs watching TV when she got up to get some tea. She asked from the kitchen if he'd like some. No answer. "Joe, do you want some tea?" No answer. She walked in and placed a hand on his shoulder. Stone cold dead! My dad said he and mom went over as soon as Grandma called, but Joe had already been taken to the hospital and pronounced dead. Dad said they would stay with Grandma and try to settle her down. Peg, or course, loved Joe and truly thought of him as a family member. She was, however, most concerned with her mother and what lay in store for her. Dad told me to go ahead to bed and then come over at eight or so the next morning. A lot would have to be done, and Barbara and I could help take some burden off Grandma and Mom.

So over I went the next morning. When I got to Grandma's house, Mom and Dad were having coffee and starting to figure out what lay ahead. I could hear Grandma's "snoring" in her bedroom.

"Let's wake her up." I said.

"No," said Daddy, "let her sleep. She has a lot ahead of her."

Well, eight o'clock became eight-thirty . . . then nine. Finally Dad said, "Well, she's got to face it sooner or later, Tom. Go wake her."

When I went in I realized the "snoring" was not like anything I had heard. It was sort of a raspy rattle. She had had a stroke or something in the night, was in a deep coma, and never came out of it. She died that day. The story made the papers because of its unusual nature. Now my mother was really in grief and shock. We had a double funeral ahead of us. With that beginning, we had the first of the two memorable events concerning these deaths and my father.

The first was Walter's decision to inform Joe Butt's adult son, Jerry, about Joe's death. Our family had never had contact with them, but Joe did have a family back in Worcester, whom he had abandoned decades earlier when he married Sophia. He essentially left Jerry and some younger siblings to fend for themselves. It wasn't our business, but my father thought the right thing to do was at least to inform them. He called them and invited them to the funeral if they cared to come. It was arranged that Jerry and his wife would arrive the morning of the funeral at the downtown bus station. I was to pick them up and bring them to the funeral home.

"How will I recognize them?" I asked my father.

"I have no idea. . . . Look for a guy who looks like Grandpa."

Well, off the bus stepped a timid-looking little guy who was a dead ringer for Joe Butt. "You must be Jerry," I said.

"Yes, he is," said his wife.

"Nice to meet you. Sorry for the circumstances," said I.

"Take us to the house," said she.

"We'll do that after we go to the funeral home," said I. "The showing is going on now, and my father thought Jerry would like to pay his respects to his father."

She grumbled; he never opened his yap.

I knew my father was only trying to be kind to Jerry, who, he realized, had clearly been wronged by Joe years before. Dad had already told me he planned to take them over to Grandma and Grandpa's home right after the funeral. Joe and Grandma had a several-year-old Valiant sitting in the garage that Dad planned to give them. He also planned to let them have any and all furniture, decorations, and other accouterments in the house—whatever they wanted, but, of course, they didn't know that yet.

My father's first concern at the moment, however, was Mother. She had not only just lost Joe, but also her beloved mother. She was really hurting. When I got to the funeral home with Jerry, I had determined that this was a unique couple. He was every inch the mealy-mouthed, hen-pecked guy his father was. The apple hadn't fallen far from the tree. And his wife (for the life of me I can't remember her name) was a total shrew! Any question I asked him, she answered. Any comment I directed to him, she fielded. When we walked into the funeral home lobby, my mother and father warmly greeted them. The "mouse" said nothing.

The "shrew" grumbled "We want to go to the house now."

My dad began to reply. "Well, I'm sure Jerry would like to pay his resp—"

"I'll tell you what Jerry wants, and that's to go to the house and grab everything we can." In so many words, she went on to reveal that they did not give a damn about Joe or his wife.

My mother swallowed. My father stiffened. I looked for a broom closet to hide in. Without even approaching the caskets (both were open), Jerry and his perky missus waited by the door to be taken to the house. I think my dad quickly concluded this was going from bad to worse, and the sooner we could get them out of there the better.

"Tom, please bring the car around. You and I will escort these nice folks over to the house right away," he said.

The house being only a block away, we were quickly there and at the front door. Dad went in first, then I. Then Mouse and Shrew. As soon as she was three feet into the living room she started. Pointing at the sofa, she said, "We'll take that, and those pictures and lamps, the coffee table and—"

"You will shut up right now," my father said, wheeling around. "You have done nothing but embarrass us and further sadden my wife. You will keep your goddamn mouth shut, and if you so much as open it to yawn I will knock it right off your goddamn face! This whole event concerns only Jerry, because he is Joe's son. We know Joe wronged you, Jerry, and we only wanted to show compassion. But you have allowed this bitch of a wife of yours to totally change our intentions. Do you have anything to say that you can actually force out of your own voice box?"

Well, other than a bad case of bug eyes, Jerry showed no reaction and failed to speak.

"Fine. I didn't think so," my dad continued. "We had intended to let you take anything you wanted—the entire household contents. But your wife's rudeness has ended that. However, in a desire to get rid of you immediately, I will offer the old Valiant in the garage. Either take these keys, get in it and head back to Massachusetts now, or Tom will dump you back at the bus station. . . . Now!"

Jerry never said a word, nor did Shrew. He meekly took the keys, they mumbled their way out to the garage and soon departed in the Valiant. We never saw or heard from them again.

That's the story as I witnessed it, but it has a more dramatic, surprise ending. A couple of weeks after the funeral, when Mom was settled down, the four of us went over to clear out the place to get ready to sell. It was a tiny, very humble abode. If I remember correctly, it sold for about $15,000 or so. Barb and I were glad to get the sofa and a few odds and ends. Most of the rest went to Goodwill. Barb and I were helping Mom and Dad take the last of the little stuff out of the house when Barb took a tacky old framed print off the wall and—whoops!—out floated $10,000! I picked up a little frayed throw rug from a bedroom floor and—zounds!—up wafted $20,000 in stock certificates. After another ten or twenty-thousand in cash drifted out of other cubby holes, we were all dumbstruck. How much more treasure lay hidden in this house . . . and where?

We proceeded to pore through every can of screws and bolts, all stacks of used and cleaned aluminum TV dinner trays and anywhere else this frugal, paranoid, old Depression Era "squirrely" couple may have stashed their "nuts." All in all, we found $80,000 in cash and stock certificates, which was a mother lode in 1968—all of which could and would have gone to Mouse and Shrew if she could have brought herself to be civil. We can only hope the Valiant gave them years of trouble-free driving pleasure!

That was the first event concerning Dad and the double deaths. The second result of these deaths and resultant $80,000 fortune had a very specific effect on Mom and Dad's future plans. Namely . . . Florida Real Estate.

With this extra cash in hand, they continued living the good life on Halesworth Road, basically forgave our $17,000 Woodstock home debt to them and also gave us a little more money for a down payment on our Sedgewick Road home in Indian Hills, North Columbus. With the birth of Wally in June of 1967, by 1968 we really needed additional space. Dad was there again with financial help and physical labor. I have a picture of Wally I, myself, and little Wally II on the patio Dad helped us build. But the main use of the extra money propelled my parents into purchasing property in two Florida locations.

The first purchase was seven building lots in a Lake Griffin development called Picciola Harbors on the north side of Leesburg. Dad had read up on the effect the coming of Disney World was to have on all of greater Orlando. He was right, of course, but Mom didn't want to live in a "too hot and too buggy" area. And as we all know, women always get their way. We ended up selling all seven lots at some small profit a few years later.

The real deal was the purchase, largely orchestrated by Mother, of a great condominium unit bought in pre-construction in the The Towers in Venice, Florida. That purchase, made possible primarily with "Gay Gay" Butt's hidden loot, set the course of our futures. And those futures were vastly different than if there had been no Venice connection.

Very good old friends of Mom and Dad, Dr. and Mrs. Jud Wilson of Columbus, had bought the rights to two Sarasota County condos, one on Longboat Key and one in Venice. Mrs. Wilson told Mom they had decided on the Longboat Key unit and Mom and Dad could have the Venice unit at what the Wilsons were paying for it—$36,000.

This particular unit was the fourth floor, southwest exposure, corner unit. Every window, believe it or not, looked out at the Gulf. In short, it was the most desirable unit in the building. My parents bought it and went into action. My father bought the aforementioned red Sea Breeze 18-foot runabout. Even though the condo wouldn't be up and "move-in-able" for more than a year, he figured you couldn't get a boat too soon. Aside from my mishap with it on the Scioto River, we had some fun with it prior to its being taken to Venice. In fact, Mom and Dad spent a couple of months of winter in Clearwater Beach, Florida, waiting for The Towers to be built.

They took the boat down and Dad had one scary mishap. He was fishing alone a few miles out in the Gulf. He said he slipped on some fish slime and basically fell backward over the side. By sheer luck he caught hold of the gunnel with both hands behind his back . . . and hung there upside down contemplating his situation. He was a 65-year-old heart patient, alone at sea, hanging upside down, outside his boat in a rough sea. Not bad . . . after all, he had caught a couple of fish . . . and his life insurance was paid up. Nope! He wasn't ready to cash it in quite yet. He flipped his legs around a little bit, tried to readjust his weakening grip, was about to try a "double behind your back twisting half gainer" . . . when a big wave came from the other direction and more or less rolled him back in the boat. Didn't even get his shoes wet! That was his story and he stuck to it. Honest to God, you just never knew . . .

The condo was close enough to completion that they went down in summer or fall of 1969 to buy furniture, purchasing it through Britton's Furniture in Venice. Dad trailered the boat down with the help of old friend Holly Bell. (Our yellow lab Holly is actually named Holly Belle of Manasota. I tell her often the Holly and the Belle are because we got her at Christmas, and because she is named after this Holly Bell. I explain he was a dear old friend of her Grandpa Chown and he was a very nice man. And it's nice to be named after a very nice person. It makes you nice. She totally understands . . . and she is a very nice critter.)

Finally the condo on Venice Beach was built and ready to move into, and the little red boat was just waiting for a serious fisherman like Dad to take control. Mom and Dad went back to Columbus for Thanksgiving and to wind up the year. Other than fighting a typical nagging winter cough and cold, Dad felt great. His successful forty-plus-year sales career was ending, and he and Mom were anxiously awaiting getting down to their "little piece of paradise" in Venice, Florida.

16

A Man's Legacy

THEIR CAR WAS PACKED TO THE GILLS AND THEY WERE LEAVING THE NEXT DAY, DECEMBER 6, 1969. We had them over to our Indian Hills home for dinner the night before as a "Bon Voyage" to send them into a well-deserved retirement. Dad and I shot a couple of games of pool, even though the cold and cough were dragging him down.

"Why don't you go to the doctor for that?" I asked.

"'Cause I'm going to bake it out on the beach in Venice," he cheerfully answered.

And then they went home. Our phone rang at about two a.m. That is always a jolt.

"They've taken Daddy to the hospital," Mom said. "He started coughing, and he couldn't breathe until they got an oxygen mask on him." She said Dad winked at her as they took him out the door.

"Well, I guess I should dress and come over and pick you up," I said. "I knew he should have gotten an antibiotic for that. Your trip will probably be on hold for a day or two."

Dr. Arnie Chonko . . . All-American

We arrived at University Hospital and were shown into the emergency room doctor's office. The guy on duty that night was Dr. Arnie Chonko. He had been an OSU All-American defensive safety a few years back, and I was kinda thrilled to meet him.

"I apologize for my father, Dr. Chonko. He is a stubborn man, and he should have gone to a doctor a week or two ago to get this damn cold taken care of. He and Mom were leaving for Florida today, and I suppose you're going to tell 'em they can't go now for several days or a week."

"No," said Arnie Chonko. "I wish I could tell you that, but Mr. Chown won't be going anywhere. Mr. Chown is dead."

Phew! We just sat there. My mind wasn't processing what my ears were hearing. After awhile, I asked where he was and could we see him. We were led into another room and there was Walter C. Chown, born December 22, 1903, and who died today, December 6, 1969, not quite 66 years old. There was Walter C. Chown, my father and Mom's husband, the guy I'd shot pool with only a few hours before, and the guy she was retiring to Florida with a few hours later

. . . lying dead on a stainless steel table. What the hell kind of a deal is this? Exactly what the hell is going on here?

We stood and just looked at him. No histrionics, no weeping, no conversation. The attendants told us we would have to go. They had work to do with him, and we had a lot of work ahead of us. Before we left I kissed him on the forehead. Although I can clearly remember that final contact with him, it was devoid of any particular feeling. Both Mom and I were numb.

We drove the 20 minutes from University Hospital to the Halesworth house in near silence. We parked in the garage and went into the house. I wandered from this room to that one. Mom went from that room to this one. We made no eye contact and said nothing. Finally, we met in the basement, looked directly at each other, hugged and started absolutely bawling. Dad wasn't here, and he wasn't going to Florida. Dad was dead, and he was never coming back.

The Heart Remembers

That was the first time in my life I ever felt the absoluteness of death. I never missed a beat with my grandparents' "double death" in 1968. But even though my father's heart attack back in 1960 gave us a warning, I guess I never actually thought this day would come. Or, if I knew it would eventually come, I really didn't know what "it" meant. Every death I was ever aware of either didn't directly emotionally hit me or didn't seem real. Actors in movies died and then appeared in the next movie. It was the finality of his death that threw me. It took me many years to get over the fact I would absolutely never see him again. My best friend, my idolized hero. I would never see, hear or laugh with him again.

Actually, I did see him one more time. I mean, apart from the sensation of seeing him in a passing car, or walking across a street, or standing up ahead of us in a line at the movie. I think everybody gets a jolt when they see someone with a posture or profile similar to that of a departed loved one. No, I mean, he came to me "in the flesh" as they say. Clear as a bell.

Barb and I were asleep in bed about six months or a year after his death. I had a sensation of someone at the foot of the bed, and I sat straight up. Daddy was standing there as real as Barbara was lying beside me.

"I want to tell you two things," he said. "I am absolutely fine and you need to stop grieving for me. The other thing is I want you to care for your mother. She will always need you."

And he was gone. And I went back to sleep. Strange, huh?

When I awoke and told Barb what happened, it seemed very natural.

He hadn't seemed "ghostly" in anyway. He looked perfectly normal and sounded normal. Just your average dead guy coming back with an "oh yeah, one more thing . . ." message. But to the best of my memory my mood slowly improved from that day on. It still took me years to really get over it (if I ever did). But my ability to plod on with my own life came back. And to the best of my ability I did—with Barbara's immeasurable help—look after my Mother until the day she died . . . 31 years later.

Dad's legacy is alive and evident today. His values, his humor, his stories remind me of the old Wyatt Earp theme song from the 1950s or '60s TV show: "Long live his fame and long live his glory, and long may his story be told."

Financially he left Mother well enough off that she was able to live comfortably the rest of her life. One interesting footnote on the "Gay Gay Butt Windfall Treasure" morphing into, among other things, the $36k-condo: at Margaret Chown's death in July 2000 at age 94, I inherited the condo. Since none of us had any real use for it, we put it in the for sale ads in the Venice Gondolier. It sold that day . . . for $360,000 . . . tax free. Amazing what threads weave through our lives from one generation to the next.

I will never be able to write down all the memories of Walter Chown the First that I have in my head. They come and they go. All I can say is he was a great guy and I was truly blessed to have him for a father. But as I've already mentioned, more than one Chown male had the good fortune to pair up with an exceptionally strong female. Bill Chown had his Mary McGinnis; Tom Chown had his Catherine Rodden; and Walter Chown had his Margaret Mathews.

17

Peg of My Heart

Here we go again with another very worthwhile woman who was wife and partner to one of our Chown men. Since I am not including myself or my male descendants in this narrative, I am under no pressure to comment on current Chown women. The past ones, however, are fair game.

I have already mentioned Walter Chown I's wife, Peg. Now let me round out her general life's story. She was my sainted mother, as they say, and she was your beloved "GiGi" . . .or Great Grandma to Lisa and Wally. And she was Barbara's usually-beloved but occasionally-cantankerous mother-in-law. She had both pluses and minuses, as all humans do, but in her case there were far more pluses than minuses. She was a world class, terrific mom.

Margaret Emily Mathews, a.k.a. "Peggy," was born in Manchester, England, on July 11, 1906. As earlier mentioned, her mother, Sophia, was a German girl sent to England to become a seamstress. There she met and married Charles Mathews and, at age sixteen, gave birth to Peg. I've already related how they came to America (Worcester, Massachusetts) when Peg was very young. I've also related how her father, Charles, abandoned them when she was probably well under ten years old. This event did not seem to have any lasting effect on her. As far as I personally saw, there was no residual anger, curiosity, or any other reaction to her father's absence from her life. She did mention he showed up once, at her high school graduation, whereupon he took her on a shopping spree for new clothes. The next day her mother returned all the clothes to the store. No hard feelings there!

Peggy was quite pretty. (I swear I'm not making this up. All the Chown women are prettier than average!) Her high school graduation picture is proof. She was about five feet, six inches tall, had blue eyes and wavy blondish hair, probably weighed 120 pounds or so at age 18.

She was also smart enough to enable her to be valedictorian of her 1925 class at High School of Commerce in Worcester. (She used to get mad when I'd say "Big Deal! You probably only had eleven people in your grade!") Her forte was writing and journalism. Judging from her yearbook, she was extremely popular.

The first thing that leaps out in her bio is what she did after high school. Similar to her future mother-in-law, Catherine Rodden Chown, whom Peg probably never met, she left home for a western adventure.

Peg's beloved Auntie Mae, Sophia's sister, was an RN in Milwaukee, Wisconsin. Plans were made for Peg to attend Northwestern University, in Evanston, Illinois, in the school of journalism. It would be a great education and not too far from Aunt Mae. But on the train ride from Worcester to Chicago, she got a telegram to continue on to Milwaukee. Plans had changed. Sophia and Mae decided it would be even better to enroll at Marquette University . . . in Milwaukee itself.

In retrospect, like Catherine before her, she trod a unique path—a young, single girl heading that far from home—alone—in 1924. It was also unusual for a girl to go to college. I have no statistics on it, but I'll bet less than ten or twenty percent of incoming college freshmen were women in 1924. And I'll bet less than ten percent of those were coming 1,000 miles or so to enroll. So right there, we can see our GiGi started off as a unique young lady.

I've already mentioned that Peggy immediately met Wally Chown. He told me he was a Big Man on Campus when they met. He had a model A Ford Flivver, all cut up and modified. He was the leader of the band he called "Chong's Melody Boys," and of course he was, in his opinion, extremely good looking.

She told me he was an over animated, over boisterous western wacko with a very high opinion of himself. She could take him or leave him. Moreover she had an engagement ring from Frank Hasset, her high school sweetheart back in Worcester.

After a first meeting somewhat similar to the first meeting of Wally's parents, Tom and Catherine (only without the lynching, thank God), Wally went to work correcting Peg's first impression of him. They got married in West Allis (Milwaukee) in 1926. Actually, they had already run off to Iowa and eloped, having a justice of the peace conduct the ceremony. Sophia, however, pitched such a fit they did it again in a Catholic church. I love the picture of them in swimming suits on their wedding day. I think they absolutely exude young, zany exuberance in that photo. I look at it and think, What optimism, what fun loving love birds. From them we spring!

For quite a few years Peg remained a stay-at-home wife. Notice I said wife, not mother. In the 1920s and 1930s it was considered a black mark on the husband's ability as a bread winner if the wife worked. Even though Wally traveled a lot in his selling career and Peggy had nothing to do but sit around an apartment, he didn't want her to have a job. The boredom drove her nuts, so she snuck a job at a department store. That ended when her chivalrous hubby found out. No work for his little lovey dovey. Can you imagine that today for a young wife with no kids?

Speaking of kids, Wally and Peg weren't blessed for quite a while by the stork. They were childless for at least ten years. The good part of that is they were free to uproot whenever needed for Wally's job when his sales territory changed, which it did fairly often. The bad news is they really wanted a family. Finally, Peg was expecting a baby in about 1936 or so. They must have been wildly excited after waiting ten years, and we can only imagine the heartache when a little girl was stillborn. Peg's grief was the main reason Wally had the East Cooke Road house, in Columbus, Ohio, built. The idea was the house might get Peg's mind off losing the baby girl. Then in 1938 they adopted Beth.

Peg probably was getting into being a first-time mother and homeowner when their next move occurred. And it was a very unusual one—the move to Indian Rocks Beach, Florida.

I've already commented on their life on the beach from late 1943 to early 1946 . . . about two-and-a -half years. As it was for Wally, it must also have been an idyllic existence for Peg—nothing to do but enjoy the sun and beach with her two little sea urchins. But the war—the reason they were footloose enough to have moved to Florida, finally ended, and Wally's job once again resumed. They moved back to Columbus, specifically to 2417 Abington Road, Upper Arlington, my boyhood home.

The years 1946 up to Dad's heart attack in 1960 must truly have been invigorating for Peg. The mid '40s through the mid to late '50s . . . maybe all the way up to the JFK assassination in 1963, have to go down as one of the true "Camelot" periods in American history. If you were white and had a half decent job, life in America was great. The early TV shows "Life of Riley" and "Ozzie and Harriet" weren't far off 1950s reality for the Walter Chown Family. Times had changed, however, to the extent that Wally changed his mind about his wife's working away from home. With his background in women's foundation garments, it was a natural for them to open a specialty shop and for Peggy to run it. They did well with it. My mother and dad opened the Peggy Chown Shop in 1950, and she ran it on a daily basis. She was one of the very few working moms I knew.

But even though she must have had some stress running the store and being a mom to two kids, it wasn't as though she was working in a coal mine. Owning and running a well-known, successful ladies store made her a recognizable person about town. As I've said, they had the store for about a dozen years. And again, in retrospect, I believe that experience further identified Peg as a pretty independent, confident and ahead-of-her-time woman.

Those Fabulous '50s

I guess more reflection on the 1950s may be straying a little off target, but I'm not going anywhere, and I hope you have the time to indulge me. Besides, this is my damn story, so I guess I can head in about any direction I want. Correction . . . I have to keep reminding myself that it isn't "my" story. It is our forbearers' story . . . I just happen to be writing it.

Let me briefly describe the period of time we lived on Abington Road, 1946 to 1959. The average home, ours included, was probably about 1500 square feet. Our house was probably three or four years old when Dad bought it in 1946 . . . sight unseen by Peg. With the housing shortage following WWII, we were lucky to get any house at all. Upper Arlington was a very nice and very new bedroom town for Columbus, later becoming quite "hotsy totsy," or as Upper Arlington was later disparagingly called: "Uppa Uppa"!

Abington Road ended one house past ours in open country. Dad actually took his shotgun a couple times in the late '40s out the front door, walked a hundred yards and hunted birds and rabbits! Peg used to laugh at the strange design of our house. The little hallway you entered from the garage had five doors entering it! The garage would park two cars . . . end to end. The coal burning furnace had been converted to gas right before we moved in, but the coal shoot was still there. The basement floor was a floating concrete slab. It had a half-inch gap around the entire perimeter, so when the water table rose too much, the floor would float. Several times we had a foot or more of water in the basement.

But Peg loved it! Almost every household was a family with kids. She made good friends with several neighbor ladies, and at least casually knew almost every family on Abington Road.

We kids ran free . . . in and out of everyone's home. Nobody ever locked doors. Upper Arlington in the 1940s and 1950s was an absolutely idyllic town for kids to grow up in. Today's families should have it so good! If any of us kids in any way got out of line at someone else's house, those parents would straighten us out. Once, our behind lot neighbor, Mrs. Secrest, came over and squealed on me for looking up her daughter Sandra's dress. I was grounded for a day or two; I was only about ten years old. I can't remember if I really did it, and if so, if I saw anything. (I hope the answer was yes on both counts.)

The point is, mothers had nowhere near the worries of mothers today. No kid's on alcohol, no drugs, no sex, no pornography, no obscene language, no kidnapings, no murderous abductions . . . none of the crap that has so many parents living in fear today. I know Mom always told me to "watch out for cars" every time I left the house as a kid. But the paranoia that is part and parcel of every mother's life today simply didn't exist in 1950. Yes, any and all of the above social sicknesses existed back then to some degree . . . but that degree was minuscule. Today, thanks to the sexual-revolution-drug-culture-spare-the-rod-and-spoil-the-child mentality, working moms and latchkey kids, and a whole host of other maladies mostly fueled by galloping materialism, mothers have way more to worry about than Peg Chown had.

Her era woman was a link between the Puritan first half of the 20th Century and the "let it all hang out" second half. Even in my high school years (1958-61) I never saw a girl in a two-piece bathing suit, much less a bikini or, God forbid, a thong! Peg and her cohorts must have found it difficult to bridge the gap from their 1910 upbringing to the 1960s libertine lifestyle so common in America. But the 1940s and '50s were still . . . very nice.

I know she and I almost never got at odds with each other in my growing up years. She and all my friends' moms demanded, and got, total respect. The men still opened doors and pulled out chairs for them, still held them lightly by the elbow as they crossed a street, and never told a really "blue" joke in front of a lady. An occasional "damn" or "hell" . . . but nothing like today. I often think of life in the 1940s and '50s . . . if you were white and on the right side of the railroad tracks that time must have been about as peaceful and stress-free as plantation life for the southern gentry before the Civil War. That was the existence Peg enjoyed at that time—at least, from my vantage point.

When Wally died, she experienced a double loss. One, of course, was the loss of him as her true love and best friend. But she also lost the above-mentioned way of life. Surely even without his death the world itself had changed for everyone. With all those assassinations, race riots, Vietnam, Chappaquidick, Watergate and the rest, a genteel era was replaced by the current coarse, rude and crude era. I absolutely thank God she didn't keep her mind long enough to know about President Clinton, a man who disgraced the high office he held by stooping so low in his personal life. I think with him the "Jimmy Stewart goes to Washington" view of public life fell right into the gutter. It became more like "Jimmy Swaggart goes to Washington." But she never knew.

She got to Venice, Florida, in 1970 as a 63-year-old-widow whose husband had taken care of an awful lot of her life. Yes, she had run the Peggy Chown Shop, and, yes, she had run the home the several days a week he was on the road. But as all widows (and widowers) find out, life is vastly different with no helpmate. She quickly adjusted, though. She joined Lake Venice Golf Course and played often and well. She played two or three times a week . . . and walked rather than using a cart . . . until about age 85. She volunteered as a "pink lady" at Venice

Hospital for eighteen years. In her eighties she also volunteered in the classroom for Barbara at Garden Elementary School. In short, she stayed active and enjoyed life. The first couple of years after Wally's death were pretty rough for her and, consequently, rough for us. But when we moved to Venice ourselves in 1973, she began to cheer up and get on with life. I am sure having Barb and me and, especially, grandchildren Lisa and Wally nearby, gave her a reason to live again. So as I said, she lived life with gusto from about age 65 up to about age 85 . . . when Alzheimer's Disease took over.

She then entered the last eight or nine years of her life, which were really sad. Actually, for about the last ten years or so her confusion was noticeable. I won't elaborate in this journal, but the progression of dementia that Alzheimer's Disease causes is heart-breaking. Peg went from slight forgetfulness through disorientation, to complete shut down. She went from not remembering who Wally had been, to not remembering me! It was terribly tragic. I'll bet I left her room at Pinebrook nursing home in Venice in tears a dozen times in her last year or two.

At the end, she was usually in a fetal position, rarely conscious. We had said our goodbyes and, truthfully, we prayed for her death. Nobody should have to be reduced to that poor excuse for living. She passed away in her unconscious state July 26, 2000 . . . at age 94! I don't know if I believe in Heaven, per se, but she sure as hell did! (Oh, excuse me.) And I'm sure she and Wally are someplace up there right now, teeing it up on some gorgeous golf course.

She was a great wife to and ardent supporter of Wally for 43 years. She was truly the "wind beneath his wings" throughout their almost storybook married life. Only Wally, of course, knew what she meant to him as a wife. By all observation I could only conclude that he adored her. I can, however, fully attest to her competence and value as a mother. She was A+ excellent.

Because my father traveled so much in my youth, I spent much more time with her than with him. She was a great teacher of life and giver of inspiration to me. I learned courage from her. Once during a thunder-and-lightening storm when I was very young and very scared, she solved that problem. She took me out into the garage and we sat on the front fender of the car (probably our 1949 Buick). I can still remember her arm around me while she explained the beauty of nature's ferocity . . . when viewed from a safe place, of course. She coaxed me into actually looking forward to the next big thunder boom or lightening display. To this day, during powerful storms, I still occasionally almost hear her voice and feel her arm around me. And to this day I love those storms.

She taught me to strive for excellence. She used to say the time was going to go by anyway, so you might as well do something useful with it. When Barbara was contemplating going back to school for teacher accreditation courses, Mom gave her that logic. Barb completed her courses and always credited Peg with good advice.

She always taught self-responsibility. Above all, accepting the consequences of one's actions was paramount. The you-made-your-bed-now-lie-in-it theory was lesson number one in my upbringing. A humorous example of that occurred years later, when I was in my mid- to late-thirties and a father of two. One Saturday when we were living in Golden Beach in Venice, Mom stopped by. She was on her way to play golf at one p.m. and stopped for a quick sandwich and glass of beer prior to her game. Lisa and Wally were at the lunch table and in rare form . . . complaining, arguing, whining.

As I walked Mother to her car after lunch I implored, "You see what they're like, Mom.

They're hooligans. They're mannerless bums. We can't get a cheerful moment out of either of them, and I'd trade them both for a new fishing rod. Are they a lost cause? What should we do with them?

She paused before getting in her car and looked up at me with a serene, angelic, smile. "You know," she said, "your dad and I went through the same with you and Beth. Now, I believe, it falls under the category of . . . your problem. I'm gonna go play golf. . . . See ya."

And in the car and to the golf course she went. I just laughed and thought God bless her, that's great!

She taught me so much about good, clean, purposeful living I guess I'd have to say she taught me everything. And I could repay her the only way children can ever repay their parents—by passing it on to my own kids. Luckily, though, both Lisa and Wally II (especially Lisa) were around her enough to observe and learn from her themselves. She was a true lady of her era . . . a fine, dignified but fun-loving gal . . . who impacted us all in a very positive way. We miss both her and her Wally . . . but I'm quite sure we'll eventually see them again.

In Closing

THAT ABOUT WRAPS UP WHAT I KNOW ABOUT THE CHOWNS . . . FROM THE VIKINGS TO THE "Venetians." As I said in the preface, there are surely lots of gaps and inaccuracies in my tale of Chown wanderings over the last thousand years. My goal has been to lay down a fairly accurate skeletal guideline for you. My dear, future clan mate, your job is to keep filling it in.

The question which burned in me when my dad died was: "Where did he go?" Where did all the great stories about him go? Not just the stories hovering somewhere in my memory, but those in the memories of so many people.

I wish I could remember and record all the great stories I ever witnessed or heard about my ancestors. I wish I knew even one anecdote about our "long ago" people. It is so important for each of us to record what we know because if we don't . . . when we die our memories are gone forever!

To me, this is all about love. I loved, and still love, my parents so much my heart aches over their absence. To my surprise but warm delight, I feel a love for Tom and Catherine and William and Mary, and I never met any of them. My devotion to my Barbara, our Lisa and our Wally and their families means more the older I get. The more I understand my past people and my current family, the more I have developed a love for you, my future Chown friend. That's why I'm writing all this down. So you'll know, as I do, these people, these stories, this love, this family . . . is us. It doesn't vanish. It is within us all.

So now it's up to you to keep it going. Not when you're 18 or 28 or 38, but some time after you've run your own race, raised your family and made your fortune . . . pick up your own pen. Write down what you remember about your mom and dad, your grandparents, hell . . . maybe all the way back to Barbara and me. The Chown family with all its tributaries is a great family. I've been proud to be part of it and am extremely proud to pass the name and heritage on to you. May it always serve you well, and may you always serve it well!

. . . To Be Continued . . .